Legal Bases: Baseball and the Law

ROGER I. ABRAMS

Legal Bases

Baseball and the Law

Temple University Press

PHILADELPHIA

Temple University Press, Philadelphia 19122
Copyright © 1998 by Temple University
All rights reserved
Published 1998
Printed in the United States of America

Text design by Erin Kirk New

♾ The paper used in this publication meets the requirements of American
National Standard for Information Sciences—Permanence of Paper for
Printed Library Materials, ANSI Z39.48-1984

Library of Congress Cataloging-in-Publication Data

Abrams, Roger I., 1945–
    Legal bases : baseball and the law / Roger I. Abrams.
      p.   cm.
    Includes bibliographical references and index.
    ISBN 1-56639-599-2 (alk. paper)
     1. Baseball-Law and legislation—United States.   I. Title.
  KF3989.A93   1998
  344.73'099—dc21   97-28823

To Fran, Jason, and Seth

Contents

Preface

As the fly ball cleared the left field fence and I triumphantly circled the bases, I knew, even as a Little Leaguer, that baseball would be an important part of my life. The competitive instincts and teamwork ethos I developed playing the game led me to the law rather than to the diamond, but baseball has remained a steady fixture in my life. To combine baseball and law in one project fulfills this Little Leaguer's dream.

As the dean of Rutgers Law School in Newark, New Jersey, I have the opportunity to teach and write about the legal process as well as attend Yankees games across the Hudson. My scholarly articles have focused on the labor arbitration process, a fascinating private system of adjudication created by labor unions and employers to resolve their disputes without court litigation. Since 1984 I have taught a course in Sports Law—first as a law professor at Case Western Reserve University, then as dean at Nova Southeastern University, and now as dean at Rutgers. My formal involvement with the business of baseball began in 1986, when I served as a salary arbitrator, resolving the disputes between the Mets and Ron Darling and the Indians and Brett Butler. I published a paper on baseball and the law in the *Seton Hall Journal of Sports Law*. As part of that "spring training" exercise, I researched many of the baseball stories that appear in this book, now expanded and refined to serve a larger pedagogical purpose.

Over the past twenty years, the business of baseball has experienced the pains of fundamental change. At each crisis point, television, radio, and print media asked me to explain the underlying legal issues to the public in language nonlawyers would understand. Free agency, arbitration, antitrust law, salary caps, Pete Rose's banishment from baseball—these stories were not limited to the sports pages. That experience in public discourse about law and baseball led to this book.

The American legal system belongs to all of us, not just to lawyers and judges. We are entitled to know about public and private lawmaking, about contracts, torts and the criminal law. It is a lawyer's responsibility as a guardian of that system to teach the public about the legal process. This book is one way in which I am trying to fulfill that responsibility.

Society passes on its culture to future generations in many ways, including—most important—through higher education. Most texts about the legal process are dry recitations, as stimulating as an intentional walk. Learning works best in an interesting context, especially one with as much inherent interest as the history of our national pastime. Baseball is tailor-made for this educational purpose, filled with colorful characters and perfect examples of the legal process in action.

I am indebted to many research assistants and library professionals for their help on this project. Most recently, Rutgers law students Ingrid Johnson and Aurora Bearse improved my drafts immensely. Elizabeth Edinger from the Rutgers Law Library and Billie Jo Kaufman from the Nova Southeastern Law Library provided indispensable resources. Many colleagues and friends read and critiqued some or all of the book's chapters, including Sheldon Leader, Gary Francione, Marie Melito, and George Thomas.

My younger son, Seth, added the great insight that only someone in the target audience with the tenacity to root for the Cleveland Indians could offer. His rich intellect is surpassed only by his humanness. Someday, Seth will be a great academic. My older son Jason's courage in the face of a disability served as a great inspiration. Jason lives as an independent adult, a grand slam on anyone's scorecard, and roots for the Florida Marlins. The 1997 World Series seven-game battle between the Indians and the Marlins (won by the upstart Marlins) was sibling rivalry on a grand scale. I rooted for a tie, impossible of course in our national pastime.

My wife, Frances, deserves my greatest thanks, both for her encourage-
ment on this project and for the three decades we have enjoyed as life partners. Together, we have rooted for the Red Sox, the Indians, the Marlins, and
the Yankees as my academic posts have moved us around the country.

As with all books, *Legal Bases* remains a work in progress. The game continues and new legal issues will arise. Part of baseball's great attraction is that
it is a game played without a clock. We can start the game today and it might
never end. For now, this will have to do as my first at bat. I hope you enjoy
your tour around the bases of the legal process as much as I have enjoyed
writing about them.

Legal Bases: Baseball and the Law

Baseball is an index to our national

genius and character.

CHICAGO GRAND JURY

Introduction

On June 12, 1939, Judge Kenesaw Mountain Landis's car led the parade down the main street of Cooperstown, New York. The shaggy-haired czar of America's Game, sporting a baseball cap, listened intently as the "Eleven Immortals" were enshrined in the Hall of Fame—George Herman "Babe" Ruth, Honus Wagner, Ty Cobb, Grover Cleveland Alexander, Tris Speaker, Napoleon Lajoie, George Sisler, Walter Johnson, Eddie Collins, Connie Mack, and Cy Young. (Ty Cobb missed the ceremony because of a train delay.) Then the judge, the autocratic first commissioner of the game, proclaimed at the dedication ceremony: "I should like to dedicate this museum to all America, to lovers of good sportsmanship, healthy bodies, clean minds. For those are the principles of baseball."

Organized professional baseball claims to be America's national pastime, and there is much to support its claim. The sport resonates with America's self-image: a contest of skill, acumen, and, occasionally, trickery between individuals who are members of teams. Baseball is a beautiful enterprise that flashing spikes, occasional brawls, insatiable greed, and various scandals can sully—much like the American nation. Baseball causes adults to grow rhapsodic about a child's game. It stimulates delight and precipitates despair. Organized professional baseball has been ravaged, at times, by an odious crowd of villains and fools, and yet it continues to rebound along with the American spirit.

If baseball is the heart of America, the legal process provides the sinews that hold it in place. It was the legal process that allowed Chicago industrialist William Hulbert to bring club-owning "magnates" together in a New York City hotel in 1876 to form the National League; and it empowered Marvin Miller, ninety years later, to transmute a management-funded fraternity of ballplayers into the strongest trade union in America. The legal process constructed both an anomalous exemption from the antitrust laws for the business of baseball in 1922 and an arbitration system that set the players free from the constraints of the reserve system in 1975. The legal process permitted owners and players almost to destroy the professional game in the mid-1990s, only later to rescue the pastime at the edge of the precipice.

The American legal process operates within a body of principles called the law, applied by a variety of governmental and societal institutions. But the legal process encompasses more than the formal structures of the law; it also includes private decision making by groups of individuals acting in their own self-interest, what the late Harvard Law School professors Henry Hart and Albert Sacks called "private ordering." In these private situations, courts, administrative agencies, and labor arbitrators often play only a secondary or facilitating role. Without the formal legal process, however, private agreements ultimately would be unenforceable and, therefore, pointless.

Lawyers have played prominent roles in the history of the baseball enterprise. Some, such as federal judge Kenesaw Mountain Landis, were chosen to serve in the governance structure of the game because they were respected members of the legal profession. Others, such as Landis's archfoe, St. Louis Cardinals and Brooklyn Dodgers executive Wesley Branch Rickey, used skills as lawyers to remake the baseball business. Other lawyers did not fare as well in shaping baseball's history. Former Supreme Court Justice Arthur Goldberg, for example, badly muffed Curt Flood's antitrust case when he argued before his former High Court brethren in 1972. A pitcher-infielder and Columbia-trained lawyer named John Montgomery Ward led a players' revolt in 1890 that ultimately proved disastrous.

How influential have lawyers and the legal process been, on and off the baseball field? Alexis de Tocqueville's perceptive analysis of American society more than 150 years ago is worth recalling:

> In America there are no nobles or literary men, and the people are apt to mistrust the wealthy; lawyers consequently form the highest political class and the most cultivated portion of society. . . . If I were asked where I place the American aristocracy, I should reply without hesitation that it is not among the rich, who are united by no common tie; it occupies the judicial bench and the bar.

The history of baseball is filled with these American "noble aristocrats"—some who practiced law, others who played law-related roles in management offices. When de Tocqueville visited the United States, groups of young men in big cities on the East Coast were developing the rules of baseball. Those rules—often texts as intricate as a securities prospectus—also illustrate the bond between the sport and the law. Only an attorney could revel in the complexities of the infield fly rule.

The baseball business presents a splendid opportunity to discuss the role of law, legal institutions, and private ordering in the development of a significant American business enterprise. This book is about baseball because the game is a mirror to our history, our identity, and our culture. Baseball is also a business and, as such, offers insight into the economics of the entertainment field.

This book is also about law and legal systems, the epoxy for this diverse country. Legal principles define rights and responsibilities in society, and they arise from both public and private institutions. Because baseball is almost a universal American metaphor, it serves well to demonstrate the operation of the American legal process. A discussion that draws on both baseball and the legal process shows the law in operation, for better or for worse. In fact, participating in the legal process may have already superseded baseball as our real national pastime.

Baseball also shows the stark contrast between myth and reality. Landis's dedication of the Cooperstown Hall of Fame in 1939, for example, was intended to commemorate the one hundredth anniversary of the invention of a sport sprung full blown from the head of an army officer in that bucolic New York village. In an early example of revisionist history, Albert Spalding promoted the Abner Doubleday myth to establish an American origin for the game, although baseball was a linear descendant of the British sport of rounders. Baseball wanted its origins to be located in a farmer's field in Cooperstown, even though they were not. Fables and fact have continued to intertwine throughout the history of the sport.

To tell the story of the development of the law and business of baseball, this book focuses on nine men and one woman who played pivotal roles in its history. They constitute our "All-Star Baseball Law Team." Some were great ballplayers, such as Napoleon Lajoie, the finest second baseman of all time. Others were not players at all, such as federal judge Sonia Sotomayor, who issued an injunction against the owners in 1995 that saved the game from self-destruction. Because this is the story of the baseball enterprise, we must have an owner on our All-Star team—actually two owners, Branch Rickey and Charles O. Finley, who share that position on our squad much as ballplayers are platooned depending on whether the pitcher is a righty or a southpaw. We also need a starting union leader, the indomitable Marvin Miller, who effectively challenged the baseball cartel.

There is one notable omission from the All-Star Baseball Law Team's starting lineup—baseball's first commissioner, Judge Kenesaw Mountain Landis. One chapter would not have been sufficient to discuss his impact on the baseball business. As baseball's brooding omnipresence for almost a quarter century, Landis's influence pervades our text. If the All-Star Baseball Law Team had a field manager, it would be Commissioner Landis.

The relationship between baseball and the legal process dates from the earliest days of the organized game, when young men from New York City ferried across the Hudson River to Hoboken, New Jersey, to play the sport on the Elysian Fields cricket pitch; they signed a formal lease contract, paying seventy-five dollars for use of the field. While there are days when many fans might wish the law and the lawyers would just go away, it is the legal process that makes the baseball enterprise possible. It secures player contracts and stadium leases, ensures that participants receive equitable treatment, and allows the sport to govern itself without governmental intervention.

This book discusses the central aspects of the American legal process, including the relationship between private and public ordering, the enforcement of contracts, the effect of precedent, alternative dispute resolution, constitutional principles, and the criminal law. I focus on labor arbitration, collective bargaining, and the role of administrative agencies. Law, legal institutions, economics, sociology, and political theory intersect throughout the text.

In the Notes section, I provide complete citations to the cases discussed in the text and point the reader to sources to further explore each chapter's le-

gal issues and baseball lore. The Baseball Hall of Fame Library in Cooperstown serves as a valuable resource for all aspects of baseball history. Collective bargaining agreements and arbitration opinions can also be obtained
from Major League Baseball and the Major League Baseball Players Association at the New York City offices.

When the Chicago grand jury returned indictments against Chicago "Black
Sox" who took bribes to throw the 1919 World Series, it submitted a report
that set baseball apart from the rest of society's institutions:

> The jury is impressed with the fact that baseball is an index to our national genius
> and character. The American principle of genius and fair play must prevail, and
> it is important that the game be clean, from the most humble player to the high-
> est dignitary. . . . Baseball is more than a national game; it is an American insti-
> tution, having its place prominently and significantly in the life of the people.

The petit jury then acquitted the Chicago players of conspiracy to defraud
the public after the confessions of two players suddenly disappeared. If baseball is "an index of our national genius and character," then for 150 years, the
legal process has been its measure.

1: The Legal Process at the Birth of Baseball

JOHN MONTGOMERY

"MONTE" WARD

The only player in major-league history
to win 100 games as a pitcher and
collect 2,000 hits as a batter, Monte
Ward, a Columbia-trained lawyer,
organized the first players union and
created the ill-fated Players League that
challenged the National League in
1890. *(Photo courtesy of National
Baseball Hall of Fame Library,
Cooperstown, N.Y.)*

The history of organized baseball and the legal process is a story

about people and institutions. This game, which means so much to America, is now a very big business, but that was not always the case. At its creation the enterprise was disorganized, almost chaotic. And from the outset, the legal process played an important role in transforming a pastime, a summertime amusement, into a commercial venture, run not by the talented young men who played the game but by the entrepreneurs who supplied the capital.

We can better understand the genesis of organized baseball by focusing on John Montgomery Ward, an important player from the first decades of professional baseball who will serve as the leadoff batter on our All-Star Baseball Law Team. Ward's failed effort to wrest control of the baseball enterprise from the magnates fixed the structure of the business for over a century. Ward's legacy—the first unionization of the players and the first and only attempt by players to operate a league of their own—makes him a notable contributor to the early history of the organized game.

Ward's promise as a baseball player was recognized early; Henry Chadwick, the first chronicler of the game, wrote about Ward in the late 1870s, when the pitcher was still a teenager. Monte Ward began his career on the mound and, like many hurlers on the small squads of that day, played outfield when not pitching. He started in seventy games each of his first two full seasons with the Providence Grays of the National League. Ward is credited with developing one of the first successful curveballs, and on June 17, 1880, he pitched one of the earliest perfect games in baseball history. In 1884, Ward gave up the mound after completing a 158–102 record and began playing infield full time.

But Monte Ward was more than just a great ballplayer. A graduate of Columbia Law School, he had attended night classes while playing for the New York Giants. He spoke five languages, wrote columns for national magazines, and in 1888 published *How to Become a Player,* a baseball book for youngsters. For his exploits on the diamond—he is the only player in major league history to win one hundred games as a pitcher and collect two thousand hits as a batter—Ward was voted into the Hall of Fame in 1964. Off the field, as the founder of the first players union and the Players League of 1890, he needed all his skills as a lawyer and a propagandist.

The Origins of Organized Baseball and the Formation of the National League

In 1876, two years before Ward began his professional career, William Ambrose Hulbert formed the National League of Professional Base Ball Clubs. A successful Chicago coal merchant and president of that city's treasured White Stockings nine, Hulbert realized that to attract fans, the sport needed a stable confederation of teams bound by common rules and schedules. The existing league, the National Association, was a loose collection of teams that accepted any entrant that could pay a ten-dollar fee. Gambling and fixing of contests were rampant.

By 1875, Hulbert had assembled in Chicago the best players he could lure from other clubs, including Boston's Albert Spalding as the White Stockings' new pitcher, captain, and manager and Philadelphia's first baseman Adrian "Cap" Anson, perhaps the best ballplayer in the nation at the time. Then, on February 2, 1876, Hulbert invited the owners of the seven strongest clubs in the National Association to a meeting in the Grand Central Hotel in New York City. Legend has it that once they all had arrived, Hulbert locked the door and hid the key. Before they left the room, these "magnates," as they called themselves, formed the National League. It was composed initially of clubs representing Boston; Chicago; Cincinnati; Hartford, Connecticut; Louisville, Kentucky; New York; Philadelphia; and St. Louis, each of which paid one hundred dollars as annual dues.

Hulbert and his fellow owners reshaped the business side of a sport that had already captured America's imagination. The game, despite its pastoral appearance—broad, green fields and dirt pathways—germinated in the industrial cities of the eastern seaboard, in particular in New York City. Sport is a primal human endeavor, with ancient origins; survival always has required teamwork, and in their games, humans have always prepared for the exigencies of life. During the 1840s, the game of "ball" served that function for young men who had come to Gotham to seek their fortune in business and who used the game as an outlet for their athleticism.

The young men of New York formed clubs, most notably the famous Knickerbockers, to pursue their athletic pastime after work and on days off. It is said that the first game the Knickerbockers played against an opponent was held on June 19, 1846, across the Hudson River in Hoboken, New Jersey, on the aptly named cricket pitch the Elysian Fields. Although fifty years later baseball's rulers would concoct an alternative orthodoxy featuring Abner Doubleday, later a Civil War general, who chased the cows off Elihu Phinney's pasture in Cooperstown to lay out baseball's first diamond, it is more likely that the Knickerbockers Club played the first game that approximates what we know today as the national pastime. But the Knickerbockers' account, too, might only be apocryphal.

Whatever its specific origins, baseball quickly became a favorite American pastime.

Baseball Rules and the Legal Process

The New York Knickerbockers regularized the rules of the game of ball, which had been played in America in one form or another for over a century. All sports must have internal understandings or arrangements that control the playing of the game. There is a need for formal rules when moral force alone cannot govern human interaction or when the spirit of sport proves insufficient to organize a structured game. Without rules, there would be chaos on the ball field; imagine, for instance, a game where one side demanded five outs per inning and the other placed fifteen players in the field.

If a game is to spread beyond a neighborhood, and if challenge matches are to be scheduled, someone must transcribe a set of rules. Written rules achieve fairness by providing a measure of predictability for the participants and spectators alike. Alexander Joy Cartwright, a bank teller, volunteer fireman, and one of the founders of the Knickerbockers, is credited with transcribing the Knickerbockers' rules. Other clubs across the country gradually adopted the design of what became known as "the New York game."

Cartwright's skeleton rules have remained remarkably stable for 150 years. The "laws" of baseball, the internal rules governing the play of the game, have evolved since Cartwright's time, but an observer of the Knickerbockers' game in Hoboken would not have found it so very different from what now transpires across the Hudson River in Yankee Stadium. Bases were set ninety feet apart, absolutely the correct dimension; a yard shorter or longer would have changed the nature of the game, making put outs either too easy or too difficult. Players scored runs, called "aces" by Cartwright, by touching all the bases and home base. The pitcher delivered the ball from his box (a term, like many, adopted from cricket), and the batter struck at it with a bat. Nine players were out on the field—although all the infielders, except the shortstop, stood directly on their bases—and nine innings (another cricket term) made up the game, though games ended when a team scored twenty-one runs. A neutral umpire enforced the rules controlling the interaction of the players on the field, although in the mid-nineteenth century the umpire, dressed formally in a top hat, was seated on a chair in foul ground between third and home. He could consult with spectators if he needed help in making a call.

The rules of baseball in some ways mirror the fundamental rules developed by society—the "law." An amalgam of custom, usage, and formal pronouncements, the law facilitates human interaction within an interdependent society, much as the baseball rules allow the game to proceed. Law professors Henry Hart and Albert Sacks explain:

> People need understandings about the kinds of conduct which must be avoided if cooperation is to be maintained. Even more importantly, they need understandings about the kind of affirmative conduct which is required if each member of the community is to make his due contribution to the common interest.

In addition, the law needs institutionalized means for enforcing those understandings and for changing them if they prove inadequate, a role carried out by the courts and legislatures. These institutions promote private decision making, the primary determinant of daily events in society. The law and its concomitant institutions establish the conditions that make possible community life and the advancement of the human condition.

We make most decisions in society by exercising purely private discretion and individual choice—for example, when to get up in the morning or what type of job to undertake. The use of our private liberty fills our days. A very few of those decisions, what Hart and Sacks called "the trouble cases," affect others in a way that requires some form of settlement of disparate interests by private means—for instance, we might decide where we should eat lunch by a show of hands. A still smaller group of conflicts are not so easily addressed. They require formal settlement either in public institutions, such as the courts, or in private institutions, such as the arbitration process.

On the baseball field, the designated umpires (until recently still dressed formally in "basic black") enforce the rules of play—the internal laws of the game. They call balls and strikes, outs and interference, and declare the infield fly rule in effect. Those rules are fixed only for a period of time, typically a season, although most have remained unchanged for a century. The participants may change the rules collectively if they prove inadequate or if alteration could enhance the quality of play.

In the business of baseball, a variety of internal and external institutions—the commissioner's office, the courts, arbitrators, labor-management negotiations, administrative agencies, and potentially even legislatures—declare, enforce, and alter applicable rules. These may be either private rules (those created by the self-governing enterprise) or public rules (those applied externally by the instruments of society, courts and legislative bodies).

Professionalization and Business

Baseball started in the nineteenth century as a pure diversion for the participants. It was not yet a commercial amusement with paying spectators, let alone the billion-dollar enterprise we have today. As it developed, baseball fed America's need for a secular religion; it was an organized and ritualized event, marked by indispensable concentration and intensity. Participants and spectators thought the game built character. As philosopher Michael Novak writes, "Sports are mysteries of youth and aging, perfect action and decay, fortune and misfortune, strategy and contingency. Sports are rituals concerning human survival on this planet, liturgical enactments of animal perfection and the struggles of the human spirit to prevail."

Civil War soldiers from both North and South, who knew something about "the struggles of the human spirit to prevail," played the New York City game to deal with their boredom during the long months of waiting for the few hours of terror that comprised the war. Returning veterans brought the game home with them to villages and towns across the United States. Thus baseball truly became America's Game.

Harry Wright, a great player and entrepreneur, realized that this pleasant diversion also was a potential business opportunity. The commercial spectacle of a baseball game could be the source of profit. He sensed that spectators would pay to see fine athletes perform at the highest levels of excellence on the diamond. He also knew that there was a limited pool of extraordinarily talented players who were not readily substitutable or replaceable.

In 1869, Wright collected premier ballplayers from around the country and paid them to play for the first all-professional team, the Cincinnati Red Stockings. Although other clubs had paid individual players—for example, an outstanding pitcher or a sure-hitting fielder—Wright's all-professional team, by paying all the players and by charging spectators to see the games, changed the game forever. Amateurs continued to play, as they do today; but the Red Stockings proved that if you played well enough, spectators would pay to watch you. The Red Stockings traveled the nation in 1869, playing all comers. The club ended the year undefeated.

What Wright could not accomplish with a single professional team was the organization of a stable league that kept out the gamblers and appealed to prevailing Victorian norms. Although professional teams multiplied, finally forming the National Association of Professional Base Ball Players in 1871, financial insecurity and "revolving" athletes, who moved from team to team, undermined the association. Most teams did not even complete their year's schedule of games. Betting was rampant and run by criminal elements who bought and sold games for a few dollars paid to key players. The business of baseball was ready for another revolutionary idea: the creation of "organized baseball."

In 1876, William Hulbert's National League brought stability to the baseball business. It allocated exclusive territories to the participating franchises.

This franchise monopoly within a national sports cartel allowed teams to charge fans—"cranks," as they were sometimes called at the time—substantial prices to attend games. A ticket for a National League game cost about half a day's wages for a workingman, much more than today's ticket prices. The prices limited potential spectators to the "better classes," who could afford to attend the games, which were all held during the day.

Hulbert knew that player salaries were the largest expense of the franchises, and that revolving players undermined fan interest. As a result, in 1879, National League owners imposed restraints on player movement from team to team. Each team could "reserve," or hold off the market, five players. Each club agreed not to negotiate with players reserved by the other clubs. The foreseeable and intended result was that a player, who did not have the option of playing elsewhere, could not demand a higher salary. "All the delegates," the *Cincinnati Enquirer* newspaper reported, "believe this rule will solve the problem of how to reduce wages." By 1883, both the National League and the rival American Association allowed eleven players to be reserved by each club. At the time, this was virtually an entire club's roster. The strict reserve system would control the movement and bargaining power of major-league players for almost a century.

Hulbert's National League innovations became the model for all professional sports leagues. For the first time, league rules effectively controlled player resources. Clubs enjoyed territorial exclusivity, without economic rivals. Any club wanting to join the league had to obtain the approval of all league clubs. No club could be located in a city with fewer than seventy-five thousand residents, in order to secure the potential base of spectators for the contests. Any club could expel a player from the league for violating team rules. The league prohibited teams from negotiating with a player under contract to another team during the season. Sanctions for violating a club or circuit rule included blackballing, which effectively ended a player's career at the major-league level.

Typical of employers at the time, Hulbert's magnates showed little concern for their players. Players were viewed as a rough-and-tumble group of men with great athletic prowess but little education and no business experience. The employers' cooperation effectively held down their players' salaries. Yet, despite their successful bottom-line approach, club owners bemoaned their financial fate from the earliest days of the sport. In fact, Albert Spalding, who by the 1880s had become a sporting goods tycoon and replaced Hulbert as the league's strongman, told the *Cincinnati Enquirer* in 1882, "Professional baseball is on the wane. Salaries must come down or the interest of the public must be increased in some way. If one or the other does not happen, bankruptcy stares every team in the face." It is a refrain that is as fresh as this morning's sports page.

The players' response to the owners' cartel also sounds familiar. On October 22, 1885, led by their star, John Montgomery Ward, nine members of the New York Giants created the first baseball players union, the National Brotherhood of Professional Baseball Players. Ward then formed Brotherhood chapters in every National League city.

Ward also published a series of articles that vigorously attacked baseball's reserve clause. The restraints on the players imposed by agreement among the owners, he said, were "a conspiracy, pure and simple, on the part of the clubs by which they are making money rightfully belonging to the players." The contest between players and owners for the greatest share of baseball's profits had begun.

The Nineteenth-Century Union Movement

The early unionization of baseball players is not surprising. The organization and expansion of professional baseball mirrored the explosive growth of American industry. Large-scale industrial enterprise was replacing the small shop, where workers had enjoyed personal relationships with their employer. In this environment, the union movement gained adherents nationwide. Its growth was spurred by class consciousness, the increasing urbanization of the population, and concerns that the flood of immigrants would lower rates paid to skilled workers unless the workers controlled the price of labor through exclusive guilds. Unions gave laborers the means to protect their wages and working conditions in an environment where employers focused only on maximizing profit.

The first workers to form protective trade organizations were artisans who sought to restrain the ability of employers to lower the cost of skilled services by routinizing jobs and hiring less-skilled workers, many of whom were immigrants who would work for lower wages. Craft unions created standard lists of prices for the piecework of their members. This economic strategy worked only when all (or most) of the employees agreed to work only at the set standards. Unions became the enforcement mechanism for price-setting agreements.

The American trade union movement before the Civil War was limited to the skilled trades, where workers shared apprenticeship training and a common skilled craft. The tradespeople worked in localized cottage industries, rather than in mass-production enterprises. To avoid the union's monopoly in supplying labor, owners would move to avoid the standards. To protect their standards, unions then had to organize employees regionally and, eventually, nationally. By the 1860s there were three hundred thousand union members in skilled trade unions, organized along craft lines.

The growth in American industry after the Civil War resulted in a new unionization strategy that crossed craft lines. Unionists founded the Knights of Labor as a secret organization of workers in 1869, the year the Cincinnati Red Stockings fielded the first all-professional baseball team. In 1886, after its spectacular victory against railroad magnate Jay Gould, the now-public Knights of Labor increased its membership to about seven hundred thousand nationwide. This was the same year in which Monte Ward formed the National Brotherhood.

Baseball players came from the same social strata as the early unionized workers—they were the "skilled tradesmen" on the field of play. Many came from the Irish and German working classes, and at least a fifth worked in saloons in the off-season. A staggering 80 percent of baseball players became saloon keepers after leaving the professional game.

It is not surprising that Monte Ward could encourage his fellow players to join the collective effort. The players knew that a typical professional career lasted only a few years. By the 1880s, a club's roster was only fourteen players. While players were paid well compared to other workingmen, their vocation could end at a moment's notice. As a truly elite group of athletes, baseball players sought to increase their pay while they were still able to play the game.

The club owners responded to the threat posed by Ward's union by tightening their control over the players' terms and conditions of employment.

Under the Brush Classification Plan, named after Indianapolis club president John T. Brush and put into effect during the off-season of 1888, owners ranked players in five categories, each with a set salary ranging from $1,500 to $2,500 annually. The players chafed under the plan, being, as Ward said, "graded like so many cattle" for the slaughter. The owners then broadened the reserve system to cover all players, eliminating player-generated movement from team to team. Clubs required players to sign a standard contract, renewable at a team's option and assignable to any other club.

The structure of the business of baseball was now fully in place: a comprehensive reserve system for players, a program of fines and blacklists to enforce league rules, exclusive territorial allocations, and standard rates of pay. Ward's unionization effort had resulted only in a tighter owner cartel.

The Players League

In 1889, Ward's Brotherhood issued a public "Manifesto" attacking the National League:

> There was a time when the League stood for integrity and fair dealing. Today it stands for dollars and cents. . . . Players have been bought, sold and exchanged as though they were sheep, instead of American citizens. "Reservation" . . . became for them another name for property right in the player.

A player either had to submit to the owners' system or had to leave the vocation in which he had spent years attaining proficiency. Ward's unionization effort had failed to change the baseball status quo. Frustrated by his lack of success in improving employment conditions for the players, Ward struck out in a radically different direction.

As the baseball clubs toured league cities during the 1889 season, Brotherhood activists met with potential financial backers, presenting a plan to create a rival circuit of baseball teams. On November 4, 1889, using ties forged through the Brotherhood organization, Ward announced the formation of an independent baseball league: the Players League. This rival enterprise would end the hated practices of the established league; it was to operate without a reserve clause, a classification system, or a blacklist.

Baseball players jumped to the new league like kids into a country pond, ignoring the promise they had made in their National League contracts not to play for any other baseball club. To give the new clubs stability, players signed three-year Players League contracts at the same salaries they had received from their National League clubs in either 1888 or 1889, whichever was higher.

The Players League's business structure was unique in the history of professional sports. Players knew they needed financial support for the venture. Encouraged by streetcar entrepreneur Albert L. Johnson of Cleveland, who wanted a baseball park on his transit line to attract ridership, businessmen flocked to the venture. The new league's financial backers, or "contributors," planned to share the profits of the league with the players. Many players purchased stock in their own clubs.

Governance of the new business venture was also distinctive. Each club had its own eight-man board, split evenly between player and contributor representatives. A senate of sixteen men, two from each of the eight clubs, half chosen by the players, half by the backers, governed the new venture. The senate selected from its membership a president and a vice president and appointed an outside secretary-treasurer.

Organized baseball's initial response to the insurrection was to turn to the courts. Monte Ward's 1889 player contract with the National League Giants contained a clause that gave the club the right to reserve him for the 1890 season. After Ward renounced his contract to participate in the Players League, the Giants filed suit in the New York Supreme Court. The club sought an injunction to restrain Ward from "playing the game of baseball . . . for any person or corporation except the plaintiff." Ward argued the term *reserve* meant only that he had promised not to play for another National League club, but Justice Morgan Joseph O'Brien disagreed. The court found, however, that the reserve clause neglected to specify the terms of his renewed 1890 contract. What was Ward's 1890 salary? What did Ward agree to do for that salary? With such central questions left unanswered in the employment contract, the court decided the reserve clause was "too indefinite" to enforce.

The Giants had asked the state court to issue an injunction against Ward. Courts recognize that the injunction—a court order to do something or not to do something, on penalty of contempt—is a powerful weapon, and that they should issue this extraordinary remedy only in limited circumstances. Courts examine the "equities" of a case to determine whether "equitable relief"—in this case, an injunction—is warranted. The New York court stated in Ward's case: "The want of fairness and of mutuality, which are fatal to [the contract's] enforcement in equity, are apparent." The court then characterized the Giants' construction of the contract as a "spectacle." Under the club's reading of the standard player agreement, the player could be bound to a club for years, but the club had an obligation to the player lasting only ten days. This lack of mutuality doomed the Giants' legal claim.

Ward's case was an early test of the enforceability of the National League's player restraint system, although it was not the first example of baseball's entanglement with the judicial system. In 1882, the Cincinnati club of the newly formed American Association had sued infielder Samuel Washington Wise for not honoring his contract. He had jumped to the Boston club of the National League before playing a single game for the Red Stockings. The Massachusetts state court refused to grant Cincinnati's request for an injunction, and Wise remained with Boston.

The outcome in Ward's case, and in others like it, signaled that the formal judicial system might not assist management in enforcing the terms of one-sided player contracts. This was a troubling development for the magnates. The long-term success of any collective business enterprise, such as the National League, depends on the enforceability of the terms of private agreements entered into between club owners and between teams and their players. William Hulbert's agreement establishing his National League assigned the clubs exclusive control over their player resources. It did not, and could not, control nonsignatories to that agreement, such as clubs in a rival league or, in this case, players who would form their own league.

The players' legal triumphs—they won almost every lawsuit brought by the National League clubs to enforce the terms of the reserve system—jeopardized the established league's business. The National League owners did not want to accept the existence of a rival league using their former players, but the courts would not cooperate. In response, the magnates turned to tactics outside the formal legal process to reestablish their primacy. Unable to prevail in courts ordinarily available for contract enforcement, they would invoke "private sanctions," such as coercion and bribery.

The Players League matched its success in the courts with sparkling performances on the field. About 80 percent of the National League's players moved to the new league. Defectors included future Hall of Famers Dan Brouthers, the nineteenth century's greatest slugger, with sixteen .300 seasons and a .417 average in 1887; James "Pud" Galvin, baseball's first three-hundred-game winner; Hugh Duffy, who later hit .300 for ten straight years, with a .438 average in 1894; and Ed Delahanty, the first player ever to hit four home runs in a game. Interestingly, two men who would become influential club owners in the twentieth century—catcher Connie Mack and first baseman Charles Comiskey—also jumped to the Players League.

The backers of the New York City franchise quickly erected wooden stands for Brotherhood Park in New York, on a site adjacent to the Polo Grounds, and challenged the Giants head-to-head for the public's attention. On Opening Day in 1890, twenty thousand patrons attended the Players League game in Brotherhood Park, while a thousand spectators watched the Giants.

The Players League followed the strategy that would come to be used by rival leagues in all professional sports. It attracted known stars from an established league in order to gain visibility and legitimacy with sports fans. Some members of the public may have perceived these players as traitors, seeking only economic gain at the expense of loyalty to their teams. But for other fans, the rival league produced more entertainment at lower prices. For an athlete with a short career span, economic reality mandated taking advantage of these rare opportunities. Even players who stayed with the established league benefited from the rivalry, finding employers willing to pay more to retain their services in a dwindling pool of available players.

The National League fought back under the leadership of the league's Chicago strongman Albert Spalding, who established a league "war fund." The magnates pounded the Players League financially, first by scheduling games in direct competition with Players League contests and then by distributing free National League game passes throughout town. Each side falsified attendance figures and pursued the propaganda war in the press. Spalding announced, "I am for war without quarter. I was opposed to it at first, but now I want to fight until one of us drops dead."

The idealistic Ward, his cohorts, and his "contributors" were not prepared for the rough style of Spalding's business play of the 1890s. Both sides suf-

fered a financial calamity, but the more-experienced National League owners prevailed. Through the use of propaganda, threats, personal intimidation,
and financial offers, the National League magnates induced the Players
League's relatively naive and inexperienced financial backers to desert the
rebel cause. Ward announced that the venture collapsed because of "stupid-
ity, avarice, and treachery."

The Players League folded after one year of play, and the National League
accepted most of the players back with major salary reductions. Spalding won
this critical skirmish in what he termed "the irrepressible conflict between
Labor and Capital." He welcomed the players back to the fold, confident that
his league would once again reign victorious: "When the spring comes and
the grass is green upon the last resting place of anarchy, the National
[League] will rise again in all its weight and restore . . . to all its purity [our]
national pastime—the great game of base ball."

Monte Ward returned to the National League, played for the Brooklyn
club for two years, and then completed his baseball career with the New York
Giants. He later practiced law full time, representing baseball players in contract disputes with their clubs.

Legal Process at the Birth of Baseball

The early decades of organized baseball demonstrate some of the various
ways in which society organizes and regulates its business activities. The formal principles of societal control—the law—allow people to resolve problems that arise when they live in an interdependent society. Nevertheless, the
law is only one of many methods to facilitate business interaction, and it is a
method with great limitations. Formal public institutions, such as legislatures
and the courts, create and apply the law, but they leave broad discretion to
private decision making. Individuals arrange the most important parts of their
life by "private ordering." Despite widespread complaints about governmental intrusion into our lives, the American system, based solidly on a private
economy and individual initiative, operates free of public interference.

Within the arena of private arrangement, conflicting interests are inevitable. Ward and his fellow ballplayers confronted what they recognized as
a privately constructed cartel of owners that imposed unfavorable terms and

conditions on their employment. In response, the players used the power of private decision making to create a voluntary organization of their own, a brotherhood of professional ballplayers. Individually, or even collectively in a union, however, the players did not have the economic power to temper the owners' unilateral control. It was necessary to pursue other alternatives.

Ward first attempted to bolster the players' economic power through an appeal to public opinion. Propaganda, an instrument of "coercion," may be effective in some instances, but the Brotherhood Manifesto had no impact. Then, as now, the public cared little for the pleas of highly paid athletes— young men who "played" for pay, rather than performing any "real work." The public cared only about their summertime amusement. Ward responded by offering them a circuit of star-studded teams run by the players themselves— something that enhanced the potential entertainment value of the sport. Ward's self-help approach imposed an even greater cost on owners than with-holding player services through a strike: not only did the players not play for their National League clubs, but they also established an economic rival that threatened the continued economic viability of the league.

William Hulbert's and Albert Spalding's National League, with its strict in-ternal rules and methods of self-enforcement, was typical of private industry arrangements of the time. Organized baseball fit the dictionary definition of a cartel: a combination of individual, private enterprises supplying the pub-lic with the same product—in this case, the commercial entertainment of professional baseball. Through private ordering, the owners set limits on their own competitive activities, allocating customers by means of exclusive territories and controlling the wages of players. A limited number of "firms" (the baseball franchises) controlled the supply of a product that had broad market appeal. Any such combination required strong leadership. Hulbert and Spalding provided that direction for the enterprise, enforcing the cartel's rules against its members and outsiders alike.

The public perceives baseball clubs as competitors; after all, the clubs chal-lenge each other on the field of play every day. This impression runs counter to business reality, however. Modern sports teams compete economically only when legal and political powers force them to do so. Without economic cooperation within a league, individual clubs could not survive, and the pub-lic then would be deprived of the entertainment they provide. With full cooperation, however, clubs can gain exclusive control over their territories, eliminate competition for player resources, and achieve the highest return on investment. Club cooperation keeps the game going year after year.

At the genesis of organized baseball, neither the owners nor the players resorted to the formal legal system to design their relationships or designate their "rights." Rather, they privately ordered their economic alliances. The owners certainly would have felt comfortable in court; as entrepreneurs, they sued and were sued on a regular basis in contract, tort, and property disputes. In contrast, the players shared with the working class a distrust of the formal judicial system, seeing courts as controlled by moneyed interests. It is noteworthy, then, that when the players jumped their contracts to form the Players League and the owners resorted to litigation, the courts would not enforce the owners' one-sided agreements. The owners ultimately prevailed, however, not through the exercise of legal rights in formal legal institutions but rather through the exercise of extralegal economic power and coercion.

In this early baseball litigation, the courts applied well-developed legal standards that had been established for enforcement of contracts. Although, as individuals, some judges may have favored the owners' interests, existing legal precedent pulled them in the opposite direction. The pull of precedent, however, does not always ensure that judicial attitudes remain stable. We will see in the next chapter how, only a decade later, the judicial approach toward enforcing player contracts changed in the important case involving Napoleon Lajoie and, in turn, further strengthened the baseball cartel.

The Players League venture failed because the effort lacked a source of reliable capital to create and maintain a major business enterprise. Because the players needed to build stadiums and meet payrolls, they turned to financial backers who were motivated primarily by profit and not by ideological zeal or a passion for the game.

Albert Spalding proved to be a better economic field general than John Montgomery Ward. Under his leadership, the National League was willing to use any method to win the economic battle. The Players League's failure became certain when its established rival moved beyond the courts to achieve its objectives. Forces other than law—greater bargaining power, custom, the interplay of private abilities, even illegal activity—often prove to be more powerful than law in attaining economic victory. The National League used all of these means of coercion, and it triumphed. For the next seventy years, the major battles in baseball would be fought in two forums: on the field, between teams of talented athletes, and in the corporate offices, between the "teams" of entrepreneurs interested in the profits to be won from the game. An organization of players would not play an important role again until the 1960s.

Montgomery Ward's off-field activities more than a century ago foreshadowed the role of the modern players union in revolutionizing the business of professional baseball. His Players League adventure ended dreams that the business of baseball could operate as a democratic, employee-owned enterprise without business proprietors. Albert Spalding wrote:

> As one who has been connected with both ends of the baseball problem—with reasonable success I may fairly claim—it has been my fixed belief that, like every other form of business enterprise, Base Ball depends for results upon two interdependent divisions, the one to have absolute control and direction of the system, and the other to engage—always under the executive branch—in the actual work of production. The theory is as true in the production of the game of Base Ball as in the making of baseballs or bats.

By the last decade of the nineteenth century, the basic structures of the baseball enterprise were firmly set. Franchise owners ran the enterprise, each with territorial exclusivity. Players were employees, bound by standard contracts. They were held to their teams by a tight reserve system, backed by threats of blackballing against "revolvers" who jumped their contracts. Baseball was assured stability, and the fans embraced the American Game.

He may not be the sun in the baseball firmament, but he is certainly a bright, particular star.

PENNSYLVANIA SUPREME COURT

2: The Enforcement of Contracts

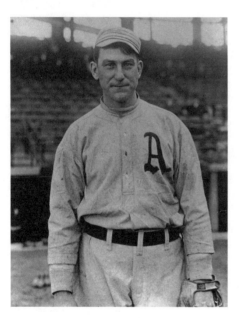

NAPOLEON "NAP" LAJOIE
The greatest second baseman of all time, Napoleon Lajoie, the "Big Frenchman," jumped from the National League Phillies to the fledgling American League Athletics in 1901, provoking litigation that would tighten the owners' cartel over player resources. (*Photo courtesy of National Baseball Hall of Fame Library, Cooperstown, N.Y.*)

The business of baseball is a collection of private contracts, understandings reached among major-league club owners and between club owners and baseball players, stadiums, concessionaires, other vendors, the media, minor-league franchises, and purchasers of the baseball "product." The uniform player's contract, securing players for each team, is the principal legal document of the enterprise. Before the turn of the century, as we have seen, it was unclear whether club owners could enforce one-sided standard player agreements in court. To stabilize the baseball enterprise, management needed to have confidence that it could compel compliance with its contractual arrangements. The case of Napoleon Lajoie, the great second baseman, gave management the assurance it needed.

Napoleon Lajoie bats second for our All-Star Baseball Law Team. The six-foot one-inch "Big Frenchman" was unquestionably one of the finest and most popular ballplayers of his time, with a batting average of .338 over a twenty-one-year career in the majors. Lajoie started his career in 1896 with the National League club in Philadelphia. After a brief stint with the new American League club in Philadelphia, Lajoie played for and managed the Cleveland Naps, a team nicknamed in his honor, from 1903 to 1915.

Lajoie's legendary exploits at second base made him an exemplary member of the Philadelphia Nationals squad, nicknamed the Phillies by local fans. He later won the new American League's Triple Crown in 1901, with fourteen homers, 125 runs batted in, and a .422 batting average (still the American League record). He also led the league that year in hits, doubles, and runs scored. Lajoie was elected to the Hall of Fame in 1937, the second year of its existence, and his plaque in Cooperstown reads "Great Batter and the Most Graceful and Efficient Second Baseman of his Era." When the shrine in

Cooperstown was dedicated in 1939, the Hall of Fame inducted Lajoie as one of the Eleven Immortals.

By the turn of the century, National League owners had agreed to impose a $2,500 salary limit on their best players, although they paid some players more money under the table. Lajoie, then with the Phillies, demanded a $500 raise in salary to match the "bonus" paid to future Hall of Fame outfielder and first baseman Ed Delahanty. The Phillies owner, Colonel John I. Rogers, a lawyer who had drafted the league's original reserve clause and uniform player's contract, summarily refused Lajoie's demand.

If Lajoie had issued his demand a year earlier, before the emergence of the American League, he would have had only two options: either quit baseball or accept Rogers's terms. By 1901, however, he had a third option: jump his contract to join the new, rival American League circuit of professional baseball teams.

The American League was the brainchild of Ban Johnson, who would dominate organized baseball for the first two decades of the twentieth century. Johnson started as a sports reporter in Cincinnati, and to get the intrusive journalist out of town, Cincinnati club owner John T. Brush recommended him for the presidency of the minor Western League. Johnson soon recognized the opportunity created by the combination of poor business leadership in the National League and the public's disillusionment with the brand of nasty baseball played by the perennial champions of the 1890s—the Baltimore Orioles and the Boston Beaneaters. When the National League dropped from twelve franchises to eight because of falling attendance, Johnson quickly established teams in the abandoned cities and placed an additional team in Chicago, Albert Spalding's hometown. He then announced that he would rename the Western League the "American League" and, in doing so, claim full major-league status. Johnson and his business partners then forged ahead to raid the rosters of National League clubs.

The Player Contract

To gain the public's attention and maintain their interest over time, every sports enterprise must secure the services of its players, particularly its stars. Clubs sign individual contracts with players that contain three important elements: (1) the player's promise to play for the team, (2) the player's promise not to play for another team, and (3) a clause allowing the club to extend the contract at its option.

Today, the baseball uniform player's agreement is the product of negotiations between Major League Baseball and the Major League Baseball Players Association. Unlike the broad terms of Napoleon Lajoie's contract, the current player's agreement covers a specified time period, or "term." A player warrants that he will keep himself in "first-class physical condition" so that he is fit enough to play during the contract term. Much like player contracts at the turn of the century, however, under the current agreement club management retains the right to terminate the agreement if it determines the player lacks "sufficient skill or competitive ability to qualify or continue as a member of the Club's team." A baseball player enjoys very little job security, although clubs never "fire" him; they "release" him from his contract, a euphemism befitting a game where myth is often as important as fact.

The Lajoie Litigation

With the number of National League clubs declining and a cap placed on salaries, baseball players at the turn of the century grew increasingly discontent. In 1900 they created their second union, the Players Protective Association. This organization proved as ineffectual as Monte Ward's Brotherhood. But Ban Johnson took advantage of the players' dissatisfaction with the National League to stock his American League, which he then claimed, with some justification, was a true rival major league.

Johnson and his American League cohorts offered attractive salaries to the most talented players from the established circuit, and the eager recruits quickly established the league's credibility. Of the 182 players on American League club rosters in 1901, 111 were former National Leaguers. Established stars skipped out on their contracts for just a few extra dollars a year. Johnson's strategy for fostering the legitimacy of a rival league—raiding the existing league—established the paradigm for success that has been followed throughout the twentieth century by rival leagues in basketball, football, and hockey.

In keeping with this strategy, young Connie Mack, the owner of the Philadelphia Athletics, the Phillies' crosstown American League rival, offered

Lajoie $24,000 over three years. Phillies owner Rogers responded with an even better deal—$25,000 for the next two years—but he would not budge on Lajoie's demand for an extra $500 for the 1901 season. Lajoie accepted Mack's offer and jumped to the American League Athletics for the 1901 campaign.

What could the Phillies club do to recapture its star second baseman? It could have sued in court, seeking an award of damages against Lajoie for breach of his player contract, but that would not have returned him to their infield. A substantial sum of money won in litigation may have been sufficient to sign another ballplayer, but players of Lajoie's caliber were not readily available, and even a century ago, litigation took time to complete. There was another problem with seeking damages: How could a court possibly quantify the amount the Phillies had lost? How many fans had stayed away from the National League club's games to attend the contests of the new American League club? Estimating the Phillies' loss would have been mere speculation.

The Phillies organization needed Lajoie's services, not his (or Connie Mack's) money. Therefore, it tried to recapture the second baseman by seeking a court order compelling him to play for the Philadelphia National League club. Like Monte Ward more than a decade earlier, Lajoie had promised he would not play for another team; but that was exactly what he had done. The Phillies argued that Lajoie was bound to the club by the terms of his partially performed contract for as long as it wanted to employ him.

The Phillies asked the state trial court to issue an injunction that would order Lajoie to fulfill his contract with the Phillies. The court's first task was to identify the relevant precedent, those general principles of law it should apply in responding to the club's request. It looked to the reasoning that other courts had relied on when they faced similar issues.

The trial court based much of its reasoning on a famous English decision involving opera singer Johanna Wagner, the daughter of composer Richard Wagner. Johanna Wagner violated her contract with Her Majesty's Theatre in London by engaging to sing with the Royal Italian Opera. The theater requested "specific performance" of her personal service contract; they wanted the court to force her to sing for them. The English court refused the theater's demand for an injunction, reasoning that monetary damages were a sufficient remedy for the breach; the court would not force Wagner to sing at the theater, even though she had promised to do so. In her contract, however, Wagner also had promised not to sing for anyone else in the same geographical area during the term of the contract—a "negative covenant." The court enforced this portion of the agreement. If the great opera star could not sing for anyone else, she would naturally choose to sing at Her Majesty's Theatre if she wanted to sing for pay. Wagner's case became, and remains today, the standard for enforcing personal service contracts in the entertainment industry.

To warrant issuing any form of an injunction, including enforcing a "negative covenant," the established legal precedent required courts to conclude that money damages could not fully remedy the alleged breach of contract and that the performer's services were truly "unique," meaning that no adequate replacement could be found.

Unlike the executive branch, the courts have no armies to enforce their orders. Their power flows from the public's recognition of their legitimacy and its willingness to obey the courts' orders voluntarily. Courts serve as society's guardian of elemental shared values, such as promise keeping. Judicial power must, therefore, be exercised with considerable restraint, lest the populace lose respect for an institution that depends on the consent of the governed for its power. Hence courts are reluctant to issue orders directing parties to act (or not to act), on penalty of contempt.

A court injunction forcing a ballplayer to play for his club would create an enforcement nightmare. How could a court determine whether the player was meeting the terms of the injunction? Apart from requiring the player to show up at the ballpark ready to play, it would be impossible for the court to know if the player was giving his best effort, which was what the employer purchased in exchange for the player's salary. Even a batting champion is rarely successful much more than one time out of three plate appearances. How would the court know if a batting slump was purposeful and in contempt of the injunction? Courts also were reluctant to compel what they considered "involuntary servitude" under a personal service contract.

The Pennsylvania state court also identified the facts of Lajoie's case. This is a critical portion of the judge's responsibility in any case tried without a jury, and juries do not sit to hear cases requesting an injunction. The trial court determined that the facts of Lajoie's case did not satisfy a crucial part of the *Wagner* test; Lajoie was not irreplaceable, not sufficiently unique or "extraordinary" to warrant issuing an injunction. Because he was replaceable, damages would suffice in lieu of an injunction directing Lajoie not to play baseball for any other team.

The lower court also questioned the fairness of certain clauses in the player's contract. For example, the Phillies could discharge Lajoie on ten days' notice, but Lajoie did not have the same right to avoid his contract obligations. The court would not place its imprimatur on such an unfair arrangement. Based on its understanding of the applicable law and the relevant facts, the trial court denied the Phillies' request for an injunction.

While the Phillies appealed their case to the Pennsylvania Supreme Court, Lajoie played the 1901 season in the American League, setting a league single-season batting record that could stand forever. But the Phillies prevailed on appeal in the state supreme court. The court ruled on April 21, 1902, that the Phillies ball club should have received the injunction it requested.

The supreme court agreed with the trial court judge that *Wagner* was the controlling case, but it interpreted the established legal principles far more narrowly than the lower court had. The petitioner still had to prove Lajoie was "unique," but the court ruled that the Phillies could meet this requirement if the club could show that their star second baseman was not easily replaceable. Did Lajoie meet this test?

The court described Lajoie thus: "He may not be the sun in the baseball firmament, but he is certainly a bright, particular star." He was part of a team that had played together for years; "he has become thoroughly familiar with the action and methods of the other players in the club." Lajoie's performance was "peculiarly meritorious as an integral part of the team work which is so essential." The second baseman was also "well known" and had a "great reputation among the patrons of the sport for ability in the position which he filled, and was thus a most attractive drawing card for the public."

The court said that Lajoie need not be one of a kind. It could issue an injunction if it would be difficult for the Phillies to find another player of his caliber in the existing labor market. The court used a functional analysis, focusing on whether Lajoie was "readily replaceable." Not surprising, it found that a replacement for the game's best infielder not easily obtainable at any price.

There was strong factual support for the court's conclusion, although it is unclear from the historical record what evidence it had before it when it reached this judgment. As a second baseman, Lajoie played the pivotal role in the double play, which, even at the turn of the century, was *the* key infield play, a pitcher's "best friend." The Reverend Billy Sunday, a former White Stockings outfielder, had said of Lajoie, "He works as noiselessly as a Corliss engine, makes hard plays easy, is great in a pinch, and never gets cold feet." In 1900, Lajoie had led the National League with sixty-nine double plays, working with journeyman Monte Cross at shortstop. It was the third year the two had paired together around the second sack.

Although the court easily jumped the legal hurdle on the element of "uniqueness," it still had to address Lajoie's claim, accepted by the trial court, that his employment contract was unfair because it lacked mutuality. This was the argument the New York trial court had adopted in Monte Ward's case twelve years earlier. Under Lajoie's contract, the club could end his employment on ten days' notice or renew his option for three years.

Mutuality, as defined by the Pennsylvania Supreme Court, did not mean that each party had to have precisely the same rights or remedies. Although the parties held very different rights under the terms of the agreement, both could seek judicial enforcement of those rights, and that, according to this court, was sufficient.

In ruling on the issue of mutuality, the Pennsylvania Supreme Court found help in paragraph 18 of Lajoie's contract:

> In consideration of the faithful performance of the conditions, covenants, undertakings and promises herein . . . , inclusive of the concession of the options of release and renewals . . . the [club] hereby agrees to pay to him for his services for said term the sum of $2,400.

In addition, paragraph 5 of the contract provided for its enforcement "in equity," that is, by the issuance of an injunction. The Pennsylvania court ignored the New York *Ward* precedent and ruled that unequal terms do not void a contract. The court said that the club had paid for its right to terminate the contract at will with a "large salary." (Although not paid as much as he wished, Lajoie's salary was, in fact, more than ten times the earnings of the average laborer of the time.)

It is interesting that the Pennsylvania Supreme Court's opinion focused on the qualities of the game of baseball and the "peculiar nature of the services demanded by the business." Baseball requires teamwork, and team efficiency on the field of play requires continuity among a team's members. At the same time, baseball management must be able to exercise discretion in determining whether a player continues to meet major-league performance standards. Thus the nature of the game requires that the team have the right to terminate the contract on short notice but to retain a player's services indefinitely if necessary.

The court was also influenced by the fact that Lajoie had partially performed his contract when he sought to leave the Phillies, that is, he had already played for the Phillies for part of the contract term. Replacing a player under these circumstances is difficult because suitable replacements may already be under contract elsewhere.

Following the *Wagner* precedent that prohibited a court from compelling someone to work for another, the court refused to order Lajoie to play for the Phillies. Instead, it enforced his promise not to play for any other club—the "negative covenant" in his contract. The desired effect of granting this injunction would be to drive the player back to his former club, where he would play baseball at his initial contract's salary.

Lajoie's case came to the Pennsylvania state courts because the parties to the contract could not resolve their dispute privately. Their private conduct—the negotiation of the contract and Lajoie's alleged breach—determined the problem they presented to the court for settlement. Courts take only the cases that parties bring to them; they do not seek out disputes to resolve or select societal problems to remedy.

The Enforcement of Contracts

As a general matter, courts will enforce contracts—exchanged promises—reached through good faith, "arm's-length," bilateral bargaining. To foster the benefits of group living and to encourage the development of human abilities, people must be able to enter into a consensual arrangement with confidence that a court will recognize the agreement and provide a remedy if there is a breach. Society values promise keeping as a way to maximize the total satisfaction of its members. It offers parties to a contract the institution of the courts as a means to enforce private agreements. Decisions to enter into contracts provide the motive force necessary for the advancement of society, and the formal institutions of society provide the stability and predictability necessary to facilitate private cooperation.

The law of contracts is a general statement of the circumstances under which courts will enforce private arrangements. Based on the reasonable expectations of contracting parties, the law does not mandate that the parties agree. Only agreements formed under certain circumstances are enforceable, however. For example, courts will not enforce contracts procured under duress. The prospect of official enforcement encourages parties to reach valid agreements and then to keep their respective promises, without official interference or institutional intervention.

Contracts between its various constituent members are omnipresent in the baseball enterprise. While the public generally knows about contracts between the athlete and his club, this is just one of many private, consensual arrangements within the business of baseball. The clubs that constitute a league are bound by contracts, such as the Major League Agreement, that allocate responsibilities and powers among the clubs and between the clubs and a governing commissioner's office. Modern baseball labor relations are controlled by the terms of a collective bargaining agreement, a contract between the Major League Baseball Players Association (the union that represents all major-league players) and the owners of the clubs for which the ballplayers play. The collective bargaining agreement has grown into an extraordinarily complex document, and as we will see, its negotiation has been the source of periodic labor strife in the latter half of the twentieth century.

Throughout its history, the baseball business has used contracts to present its form of commercial entertainment. Clubs contract with stadium owners, vendors of goods, and providers of services. Spectators contract to see the game, purchasing a ticket for entrance (unless, as happened in the early days, the "cranks" climb over or under the fence). Even at the sport's inception on the Elysian Fields, it was a lease contract that allowed the young men from New York City to play baseball on the heights of Hoboken.

To create a valid and enforceable contract between two parties, there must be an "offer" by one party and an "acceptance" of that offer by the other. In addition, there must be "consideration" to make the arrangement binding—normally a payment of some kind. This bargained-for exchange signals that the arrangement is more than a one-sided promise or gift.

The Pennsylvania Supreme Court's decision in *Lajoie* completely disregarded the manner in which ballplayers entered into contracts with their clubs. Lajoie's agreement, the basis for the club's petition to the court, was not a negotiated document. Instead, it was a "contract of adhesion," a standard form that the player could "take or leave." Even the salary was nonnegotiable, the result of the collusive arrangement among the league's magnates. Unlike the paradigmatic contract, this was not the product of genuine bilateral bargaining, with a result acceptable to both parties.

A contract imposed by one party on another lacks a consensual basis. Allowing an agreement reached as the result of duress or "undue influence" to be enforced in court gives the bully the advantage of the imposed terms. Lajoie's contract was the league standard, containing boilerplate language included in all player contracts. Signing the contract was not the result of meaningful choice on his part but rather the consequence of a gross inequality of bargaining power. Society cannot value such arrangements, and courts generally do not enforce such imposed contracts.

The state court was correct, however, that two parties to a contract do not have to possess exactly the same rights to enforce the contract's terms. The law does not limit enforcement to "balanced" or "fair" contracts, as long as they are agreements that flow from genuinely bilateral action. But in Lajoie's case, this contract of adhesion should have raised greater judicial concern, even at the turn of the century. Lajoie had no choice but to accept the terms as tendered by the Phillies, if he wanted to play baseball at the major-league level.

None of the participants in this dispute was without fault. Whatever his justification—and here it was personal greed—Lajoie broke his contractual commitment to the Phillies. Although unhappy with its terms, he knew he was bound to his contract, yet he cavalierly ignored his promises. The upstart Athletics were tainted as well; the club had sought to benefit financially at its stadium's turnstiles by interfering with an existing contract between a star player and his team. All enterprise depends on the integrity and enforceability of contracts. Considered as a whole, then, the Pennsylvania Supreme Court's result in Lajoie's case may have been an appropriate balancing of all the equities.

Lajoie's was not the only case arising out of the American League raids on National League rosters. Other state courts, however, followed the *Ward* precedent and denied injunctive relief to the clubs that lost their players to the rival league. In a 1902 Missouri case, the court referred to a player's rights under a reserve clause as "bound as with bands of steel." Yet because of his prominence and extraordinary American League performance in 1901, Lajoie's very visible case marked an important turning point in the development of the baseball cartel.

The State and Federal Court Systems

Many of our Baseball Law All-Stars have played out their roles within the judicial system. It is useful, then, to discuss briefly the complicated American court system, a confusing crazy quilt of state and federal, trial and appellate courts.

Each state has its own court system. State trial courts hear all types of civil and criminal cases and thus are courts of "general jurisdiction." One or two levels of appellate courts hear appeals from the trial level.

Different states call their trial and appellate courts different names. The Phillies sued their star infielder in the Pennsylvania state trial court, called the "court of common pleas." By comparison, the trial court in New York State is called the "supreme court," though in most states the supreme court is the highest state appellate tribunal. New York calls its highest appellate tribunal the "court of appeals."

The federal trial and appellate courts—the district courts and the U.S. courts of appeals, respectively—may hear only cases involving either federal law or state law where the litigants are from different states. The nation is divided into twelve circuits, each covering more than one state, and the court of appeals for a given circuit determines the federal law in its states. As may be imagined, there sometimes is conflict between the circuits in interpreting principles of federal law. The United States Supreme Court is the only court with jurisdiction to resolve those conflicts.

The United States Supreme Court hears appeals from both state and federal courts. The court most often selects cases that present important issues on which federal appellate courts conflict. Parties petition the Supreme Court to hear their cases, requesting a "writ of certiorari" to bring the record of the case to the Supreme Court. The Supreme Court practice is to grant "cert," as lawyers coin it, if four of the nine justices vote to hear the case. The Supreme Court accepts fewer than 2 percent of these requests.

The Curious Aftermath to *Lajoie*

The Lajoie case was crucial to the development of the modern professional baseball enterprise and baseball jurisprudence. The decision established that a professional baseball player was presumptively unique, a finding that justified equitable relief through the issuance of a negative injunction. The second baseman's case showed that courts would uphold one-sided uniform player contracts, the core of baseball's personnel system.

The Lajoie case solidified the established league's control over its players. The negative injunction enforcing the covenant not to play for another team allowed a league to implement contractual restraints on player movement not only within the league but between leagues. The Lajoie precedent fortified the league's ability to allocate player resources to meet its needs while dominating the player market.

The story has a peculiar ending for Napoleon Lajoie, however. After the Pennsylvania Supreme Court decision, Lajoie could not play for a club other than the Phillies. Frustrated by the injunction, the Philadelphia Athletics traded Lajoie to the American League entry in Cleveland, then nicknamed the Blues for their bright-colored uniforms. The Phillies then sought to enforce the Pennsylvania injunction in the Ohio state courts. Under Article 4, Section 1 of the U.S. Constitution, a state must give the judgment of another state's court "full faith and credit," that is, the same effect the decision would have in the state that rendered it. Despite this well-established, constitutionally mandated doctrine, the Ohio court refused to enforce the Pennsylvania state court injunction—a truly remarkable judgment.

The injunction against Lajoie remained in force in the Commonwealth of Pennsylvania, however. When the Cleveland team traveled to play the Athletics in Philadelphia, Lajoie avoided the effect of the injunction by going to Atlantic City, New Jersey, for vacation.

Ban Johnson's American League prospered, outdrawing the moribund National League. The economic success of the American League, the diminished profitability of the National League, and the realization that cooperation between the circuits could produce profits for all of organized baseball brought the two rival leagues to the bargaining table to negotiate a business truce. Within a year of the Lajoie decision, the American and National

Leagues signed the National Agreement, ending the war between the circuits. The National Agreement pledged "to perpetuate baseball as the national game of America, and to surround it with such safeguards as to warrant absolute public confidence in its integrity and methods." The National Agreement ushered in an era of hegemony for organized baseball, broken only by the brief rivalry of the Federal League in 1914 and 1915. Three decades of club relocations in professional baseball had ended by 1903, and the eight franchises of each circuit of the major leagues would remain in their home cities for the next half century.

Upon the signing of the National Agreement, Lajoie was free to play when his Cleveland club, renamed the Naps in his honor, came to Philadelphia. Lajoie was always a fan favorite. His contest with Ty Cobb for the American League batting crown in 1910 is legendary. By then, Cobb had earned the disdain of his fellow players, while Lajoie was well liked. The winner of the American League batting title would receive a new Chalmers automobile, and Cobb publicly vowed to prevail. Ahead of Lajoie by a few percentage points in the batting race, Cobb sat out the last few games of the season, confident in winning. During a season-ending doubleheader against the St. Louis Browns, Lajoie went eight for eight, including seven bunts laid down in front of rookie third baseman Johnny "Red" Corriden, who had been instructed to play deep. Collusion could never be proved, yet it was obvious to all observers that the players wanted Cobb to lose. He did not. He prevailed by less than a point over Lajoie. The car manufacturer recognized a good public relations opportunity and awarded the public's choice, Napoleon Lajoie, an automobile as well. (Later recalculation showed that Lajoie—with the aid of his "remarkable" series of bunt singles—had actually beaten Cobb.)

The terms of the National Agreement of 1903 are typical of league charters. It was the "constitution" of the sport. The two league presidents and a third person selected by the two, Cincinnati owner August "Garry" Herrmann, made up the National Commission that governed the business of baseball. The owners gave the tripartite National Commission the power to control the enterprise "by its own decrees," to enforce those decrees without the aid of law, and to answer to no power outside its own. In reality, however, American League president Ban Johnson ruled both the commission and the organized game until the 1920s.

The National Agreement contained no provision for a championship series. Championship series had been played periodically during the nineteenth century between the pennant winners in the National League and the
American Association. In 1903 the American League champion Boston Pil-
grims and the Pittsburgh Pirates scheduled postseason contests hyperboli-
cally termed the "World Series." Boston prevailed, five games to three.

In 1904 the American League Boston franchise, now known as the Bean-
towners, challenged the National League pennant-winning New York Giants
to a postseason series, but John T. Brush, now the owner of the Giants, declined, deriding the junior circuit as a "minor league." The New York populace was outraged, wanting more baseball—and the opportunity to trounce
the Boston nine. Brush changed his mind, but too late for the 1904 season.
In a letter to the president of the National League, Brush proposed procedures to govern a future, annual "World Series." The major leagues formally
adopted the "Brush Rules" in 1905. They were in place in time for Brush's
Giants to defeat Connie Mack's Philadelphia Athletics four games to one in
the 1905 World Series.

Baseball is, in a very distinct sense,

an exception and an anomaly.

JUSTICE HARRY BLACKMUN

3: Baseball's Antitrust Exemption

CURT FLOOD

Curt Flood wrote to Commissioner
Bowie Kuhn, "I do not feel I am a piece
of property to be bought and sold
irrespective of my wishes," and brought
suit to invalidate the reserve system
under the antitrust laws. Although his
action failed, Flood was a champion of
the players revolution who would not
compromise his principles or his
dignity. (*Photo courtesy of National
Baseball Hall of Fame Library,
Cooperstown, N.Y.*)

For sixty-seven years, players and owners cohabited the sport of base-ball according to the rules set by the 1903 "peace treaty" between the American and National Leagues. To some, this was baseball's golden era, when the sport enjoyed a monopoly on the public's attention. Basketball and football had yet to impact on the national consciousness, and hockey was a regional sport, played only by Canadian nationals. To others, however, baseball was a one-sided enterprise in which players toiled for modest salaries and then were discarded by club owners at will. This situation would change, however, as players used the legal process and formed a strong and stable union.

In 1970, Curt Flood—a great baseball player, though not of the same cal-iber as Ward or Lajoie—brought suit against organized baseball, claiming that baseball's reserve system, the owners' rule that prohibited Flood and all other baseball players from working for the employer of their choice, violated the nation's antitrust laws. Flood's suit marked an important turning point in the relationship between baseball and the legal process, and as a result, he has earned a spot on our All-Star Baseball Law Team. Although his suit was ultimately unsuccessful, Flood's courage symbolized a change in player atti-tudes that led inexorably to the demise of the venerable labor system that had allowed the baseball cartel to maintain unilateral control over players and their salaries.

The Economics of the Reserve System

As we have seen, the founders of organized baseball created the reserve sys-tem in the late 1870s. The National League magnates first agreed that each club could "reserve" five players on its roster, and the owners agreed not to tamper with other clubs' players. (Rosters at the time rarely had more than ten or eleven players; thus reserving five players secured roster continuity and controlled the market for player services.) After a few years, the owners extended the reserve system to cover each club's entire roster.

The effect of the reserve system on player salaries was dramatic. Salaries and benefits constituted as much as 60 percent of revenue before the National League adopted the reserve system. That percentage declined gradually to below 15 percent on average, for major-league clubs in the mid-1950s. With the dismantling of the reserve system in the mid-1970s (a story we detail in Chapter 6), the percentage of salary and benefits increased to 28.2 percent of revenue in 1978, 42.8 percent in 1984, and an estimated 54.9 percent in 1994 (had that season not ended early because of the players strike).

Without question, a secure and stable reserve system made good economic sense for the owners. To achieve the highest return on investment, all business owners seek to increase market power and diminish costs for employees, materials, and facilities. Player salaries potentially make up the largest segment of a baseball club's budget, and thus it was—and is—important to keep player salaries under control. Of course, reducing salaries too much can affect worker morale and productivity, increase turnover and training costs, and prevent the business from bringing its product to the market with quality sufficient to attract purchasers at a profit-making price. For major-league baseball, however, except for a few true stars, there has always been an adequate supply of substitute ballplayers in minor or amateur leagues.

A stable reserve system required the active participation of all club owners. The prevailing mandate was sports competition "on the field" but economic cooperation "off the field." In addition to creating a standard form contract that all players would sign, owners pledged not to deal with any player under contract or reserved by another club. The owners knew competition in a free market to sign talented athletes would only increase salaries and decrease profits. Unless the acquisition of star ballplayers increased attendance and produced profit above the marginal increase in player salary costs—always an uncertain prediction—it was better, on the whole, to hold down all player salaries through a universal restraint.

Under the reserve system, the contract of a player who signed with a club was that club's property for as long as he played baseball or until his employer assigned his contract to another club or, alternatively, "released" the player. The reserve system substantially diminished a player's bargaining power, because no other team could bid for his services. Clubs retained total control over the player market. A club could exercise its option to renew a player's contract in perpetuity. Alternatively, it could sell his contract to another club for the duration of his career. Either way, the player's options were limited to playing within the reserve system or not playing professional baseball at the major-league level.

Although concerned with how the reserve system diminished a player's bargaining power during salary negotiations, Curt Flood was principally challenging the power-dependency relationship established under baseball's employment system. He chafed at being forced to leave the game he loved and played so well if he did not report to another club against his will. His concerns paralleled those first raised by John Montgomery Ward and the Brotherhood of the 1880s. A baseball player under the reserve system did not have the prerogative, enjoyed by other workers, to choose an employer. He was not a person but a commodity.

Economists label the reserve player system a "monopsony," a labor market dominated by one employer. When a player is bound to a lifetime option with one club, he has only one possible employer, only one purchaser for his services. In this instance, the employer was a member club of a private cartel. Clubs exploited the monopsony when they earned more from the player's contributions to the enterprise—for example, from his ability to attract paying fans—than they paid the player. Through the monopsony, clubs could adjust player salaries to protect profitability.

Alternatively, a club could profit by selling a player's contract to another club, which then would have exclusive rights to contract with the player. Without universally recognized and enforced restrictions on player movement from team to team, the player would reap the benefit of this market exchange. Hence, the reserve system determines which party—the player or his old team—captures the increment that a new team is willing to pay to obtain the services of an experienced major-league player.

It is not easy to maintain a private cartel controlling player resources, especially one with as many members as the major leagues. To manage baseball's business, the owners needed strong central leadership. This was first provided by William Hulbert and Albert Spalding in the nineteenth century, then by Ban Johnson through the first two decades of the twentieth century, and finally by Commissioner Kenesaw Mountain Landis and his successors until the 1970s.

When the only threat to the cartel came from a maverick club owner, baseball's leadership could control the dissident by nullifying any contracts he had made in violation of major-league rules and by issuing fines. Rival leagues, such as the Federal League venture of 1914–1915, created a greater challenge, especially if the economic rivals could attack the trade practices of the major leagues under the nation's antitrust laws. In fact, however, no challenge to the cartel succeeded until the players formed a strong trade union in the late 1960s, as a countervailing power to that of the owners.

The Antitrust Paradigm

In 1890, federal district court judge William P. Wallace, quoting from "a recent publication edited by a prominent professional player" (undoubtedly, Albert Spalding), explained the absolute necessity for baseball's reserve system and the business's need for collusion:

> To this [reserve] rule more than any other thing does base-ball, as a business, owe its present substantial standing. By preserving intact the strength of the team from year to year, it places the business of base-ball on a permanent basis, and this offers security to the investment of capital. The reserve rule itself is a usurpation of the players' rights, but it is, perhaps, made necessary by the peculiar nature of the ball business, and the player is indirectly compensated by the improved standing of the game. The reserve rule takes a manager by the throat and compels him to keep his hands off his neighbor's enterprise.

Also in 1890, however, Congress enacted the Sherman Antitrust Act, prohibiting "any contract, combination or conspiracy in restraint of trade." This law presented a potentially significant problem for baseball's reserve system, which was, after all, an arrangement designed to eliminate competition between clubs for player services. Under the Sherman Act, the federal government could seek to prohibit illegal collusion; and after 1914, with Congress's passage of the Clayton Antitrust Act, private parties could sue to recover for damages caused by anticompetitive conduct. If the allegations were proven, the federal court would then treble the damages, under the terms of the statute.

The Sherman Act was Congress's response to the excesses of American business combinations and monopolies at the end of the nineteenth century. The antitrust laws also reflect deep-seated American beliefs in individualism and economic competition. Valuing entrepreneurial initiative, the legal system fosters the making of contracts by providing the means for enforcing them (as we discussed in Chapter 2). At some point, however, contracts interfere with the ability of potential competitors to enter the marketplace, thereby "restraining" trade. For example, a contract among competitors that limits the availability of raw materials may make it economically impossible for others to enter the manufacturing business. Contracts among competitors to set prices or to control or reduce production disturb the free market flow of goods and ultimately increase the retail price of products. Monopolistic and oligopolistic practices affect the prices buyers pay for products, driving them up to the point where purchasers will substitute other similar products or forgo them completely. Competitive markets, by contrast, reduce prices to the lowest level where profit can still be made.

Some restraints on trade are "horizontal," among economic players at the same level of the marketplace. For example, competitors may agree to sell goods only at a preset (and, presumably, profitable) price. Restraints may also be "vertical," imposed by an economic player on another enterprise at a different level of the marketplace. For example, a manufacturer may attempt to control the price at which a retailer may sell a good or may require the retailer to sell only the manufacturer's product. If the manufacturer enjoys sufficient economic power (or has an allocated market by an agreement among fellow manufacturers), a retailer may have no choice but to comply.

By outlawing business combinations that restrain trade, Congress sought to achieve a balance between rewarding industrious capitalists with the freedom to enter into contracts that would be enforced in court and maintaining fluid and efficient markets for goods and services. Under the antitrust laws, the free market model would regulate American business. Congress used what Hart and Sacks call a "general directive arrangement," a law applicable to all persons and entities, rather than one targeted to the practices of specific parties. Congress appreciated that its regulatory arrangement contained gaps and uncertainties and recognized a need for some entity to fill those gaps authoritatively and resolve uncertainties as individual cases arose. Under the Sherman and Clayton Acts, courts serve as Congress's enforcement mechanism, at the behest of government prosecutors or private parties who allege economic injury caused by collusion in restraint of trade. Although the formal legal system is available to enforce private arrangements, it will also nullify agreements targeted by legislative proscription as contrary to public policy. The fact that the courts enforce general directive arrangements enacted by legislatures makes it more likely, of course, that private parties will abide by the legislative pronouncement on their own, without need for official enforcement.

The legislative antitrust edict was broad and all-inclusive, barring any "contract, combination or conspiracy in restraint of trade or commerce." The courts never applied it literally, because it would have led to the absurd result of outlawing virtually all commercial contracts. Every time two businesses reach an agreement, it affects others who may have wanted to make the same arrangement with either of the two parties, especially if the amount of a product is limited. Hence the courts early on held that the antitrust laws prohibited only "unreasonable" restraints on trade, a determination made on a case-by-case basis, balancing the anticompetitive effects of the restraint with the economic justifications for the arrangement. Some restraints, such as price-fixing, are always unreasonable. Courts treat them as per se violations of the antitrust laws, without inquiry into any purported justifications.

The antitrust laws certainly covered an agreement between purchasers of worker services not to compete for employees—an agreement, as Judge Wallace said, that "takes a manager by the throat and compels him to keep his hands off his neighbor's enterprise." This was precisely the purpose and effect of baseball's reserve system.

Justifications for the Reserve System

Whenever challenged, sports franchise owners, the beneficiaries of the reserve system, have explained the system's benign purposes and social benefits—most important, the enhancement of the league's competitive balance on the field. They assert that in a free market for player services, rich teams from the larger markets would stock their rosters with the most talented players, leaving the remainder of the player pool for the clubs from smaller market cities. The resulting uncompetitive sports contests would diminish fan attendance and interest in both advantaged and disadvantaged cities. Competitive games and exciting pennant races—two products of the reserve system, according to franchise owners—serve the public's interest by providing attractive commercial amusement.

The facts, however, do not support sports team owners' claims that a reserve system maintains competitive balance. Under the comprehensive reserve system, baseball had a history of dynastic, ruling clubs—Baltimore and Boston in the 1890s; the three New York City teams throughout much of the twentieth century, until the 1960s; and the St. Louis Cardinals organization in the 1920s, 1930s, and 1940s, under the brilliant management of Branch Rickey. And some baseball clubs have remained perennial losers—the Chicago Cubs have not won a World Series since 1907, the Boston Red Sox since 1918, and the Cleveland Indians since 1948. The reserve system did nothing to enhance the competitiveness of these clubs. In fact, the only period of true on-field competitiveness in major-league baseball history has occurred since the reform of the reserve system, a story examined in Chapter 5. Since the demise of the comprehensive reserve system, many free agents have moved to clubs that generate larger revenues, in particular George Steinbrenner's New York Yankees. Yet in the decade between 1978 and 1987, ten different teams won the World Series.

Throughout baseball history there have been both rich and poor clubs. Although the reserve system allowed clubs with good management to prosper, clubs with poor management or smaller markets faltered. Defenders of the reserve system claim that, in its absence, rich clubs in major markets will sign the most talented players as free agents; but ironically, that is exactly what happened under the reserve system. To survive financially, poor clubs sold rich clubs the contracts of their better players. Without a reserve system, of course, the poor clubs would not have had the power to sell player contracts, any more than one business could sell its lead employees to another company.

Owners also suggest that the reserve system protected their substantial investment in their players. Teams expend millions of dollars annually on scouting for prospects and developing their potential in the minor leagues. Unless a team has some assurance that this investment was protected, the argument goes, the club will not expend these resources. No other industry warrants such special treatment, however. All employers depend on developing new talent—at some risk to the employer—to serve their business interests.

It is possible that the strict reserve system did increase the total revenue of the baseball industry, and the owners (and not the players) captured the profit increment. It also brought order to the business. According to Commissioner Bowie Kuhn, testifying in Curt Flood's case, the "entire climate was extremely evil" in baseball before the advent of the reserve system; "profitability was very low." A stable labor relations system under employer control fostered the marketing of the product to potential customers.

There can be no question that the reserve system served the interests of the employers. Although the few hundred major-league athletes might object, why should the public care who became rich and who did not? The public did care about the game, however, and under the strict reserve system, spectators could rely on the stability of their amusement—a social "good" by any measure.

Does baseball need a reserve system because of the nature of the game? Certainly, player continuity enhances the quality of play. Roster stability is important in a team sport, and this would justify a reserve system limited to key skilled players (shortstops and second basemen, for example) for a finite period of time. But the needs of the game simply do not justify a reserve system that covers every player for his entire professional work life. Moreover, under the comprehensive reserve system, owners did not use their power to maintain career-long roster stability. Players generally spent their careers with a variety of teams, as club management exercised its discretion to assign player contracts to other clubs.

Player continuity also enhances fan interest, and player turnover diminishes fan allegiance. If fans doubt a player's loyalty, they also may question his effort. But again, this concern may warrant a limited reserve system but not the career-long, rosterwide system maintained by organized baseball for almost a century.

Although the reserve system was broader than necessary to achieve roster stability, a high level of player performance, and the marketing of the sport, it may have been difficult for the major leagues to administer anything less than a comprehensive system. An effective monopsony maintained by a private cartel requires easily understood rules to facilitate self-policing. To leave enforcement to a case-by-case evaluation of whether a personnel move benefits the enterprise would be chaotic. On rare occasions, the commissioner has exercised discretion to nullify player movements as not in the "best interests of baseball" (we discuss examples in Chapter 5) but stability within the enterprise requires that these interventions be the exception and not the rule.

Baseball's reserve system, with certain modifications, might well have survived scrutiny under the antitrust laws. Certainly, courts were not eager to rule against the magnates on one of the core elements of their enterprise. As events unfolded, however, courts would never have the opportunity to determine if the reservation of baseball players was an unreasonable restraint of trade.

The Federal League and *Federal Baseball*

The baseball antitrust story began in 1914 with the creation of the Federal League, the last significant challenger to the major leagues' hegemony over professional major-league baseball. Following the model of Ban Johnson's American League, the Federal League began as a "minor" league in 1913. In August of that year, it announced plans to add new clubs in Buffalo, Baltimore, and Brooklyn, to complement its existing clubs in Chicago, St. Louis, Pittsburgh, Indianapolis, and Cincinnati. The league also announced its interest in attracting stars from the major leagues. With the financial support of wealthy businessmen at a time when the baseball business was a very profitable enterprise, the Federal League was prepared to contest the American and National Leagues for the public's entertainment dollars.

There had been other "outlaw" baseball leagues, including the Pacific Coast League, the Tri-State League, and the California State League. The threats they posed were quickly abated by a combination of personal entreaties and financial inducements from the major leagues, buttressed by warnings of blacklisting and fines against players who might jump their contracts. Although these smaller, regional leagues continued to exist, they agreed not to compete for major-league talent, and they ultimately became signatories to the National Agreement.

The 1910s were again a time of unrest among major league players. Ty Cobb made headlines when he held out for a higher salary before starting the 1913 season. The Players Fraternity, the third unionization effort of the players, had proved largely ineffective in protecting player interests, despite a strike threat in 1914 after a meeting in Cincinnati with major-league officials. It seemed a propitious moment for the creation of a rival league.

The Federal League presented a substantial challenge to the established leagues' control over the player labor market, much as the Players League, the American Association, and the American League had earlier rivaled the National League. The presence of other potential employers in the market created alternative opportunities for the players, breaking the tight economic grip of the reserve system monopsony and driving up player salaries in the established circuits.

The Federal League adopted a unique form of organization. The teams collectively formed into a single corporation, with stock divided among club owners, each of whom posted a $25,000 bond and transferred to the league the lease to its ballpark. To entice players to defect from the major leagues, the Federal League offered signing bonuses and a less restrictive labor relations policy. Management assured players a 5 percent annual salary increase and free agency after ten years. At the same time, Federal League rules prohibited signing any player still under contract with a major-league club. The major leagues, in turn, responded that they would blacklist any players who jumped, regardless of whether they were under contract, because they were bound by the perpetual reserve system.

The first significant defector to the Federal League was shortstop Joe Tinker, who returned from Cincinnati to manage the new league's entry in Chicago, where his exploits starting the Tinker-to-Evers-to-Chance double play had become part of the Cubs mythology. Hal Chase, Russ Ford, and Mordecai "Three Finger" Brown followed suit. In total, during its two years of play the Federal League attracted eighty-one major leaguers.

Once again, major-league magnates brought suits against the defectors, and they achieved a few victories in cases where players had breached their contracts midterm. The courts generally refused to issue injunctions against the players when clubs relied only on the reserve system's option clause as the basis for their claims. (The option clause allowed a team to renew an expired player contract annually on the same terms.) The clubs were not helped by the fact that George Wharton Pepper, the major leagues' attorney, and Garry Herrmann, the chairman of the governing National Commission, had both stated that the reserve system was an internal mechanism designed to keep major-league teams from stealing players from other major-league clubs, and that it did not keep a rival league from signing a player no longer under contract.

Many players used the leverage of a rival purchaser for their services to their economic advantage in bargaining with their major-league clubs. The clubs purchased the loyalty of their players with higher salaries, bonuses, and long-term contracts. The salaries of premier players more than doubled in one year. Some players, such as Washington's star pitcher Walter "The Big Train" Johnson, jumped to the Federal League and then back to the major leagues, increasing their salaries with each move.

Federal League owners adopted their own litigation strategy to support their business challenge to the established circuits. In January 1915, they sued the major leagues and the three members of the National Commission in federal court in Chicago under federal antitrust laws. They claimed the established structure of the baseball enterprise was a conspiracy and a monopoly. The presiding judge was Kenesaw Mountain Landis, who would soon become the most prominent figure in the business of baseball.

Landis had developed a reputation as a "trustbuster," which was why the Federal League brought its suit in his court. Apparently, however, the Federal League owners did not know that Landis was also an avid major-league baseball fan. Imagine the plaintiffs' consternation when Landis announced in court that "any blows at the thing called baseball would be regarded by this court as a blow to a national institution." Landis was true to his word and took the case under advisement for a year. He also had passed the audition that would later lead to his appointment by major-league owners as the first commissioner of baseball in 1920.

While Landis stalled the antitrust litigation, Federal League attendance suffered. By 1915, the rival owners began to meet secretly to discuss peace. Finally, on December 13, 1915, at dinner at the Republican Club in New York City, they struck a deal that they finalized four days later at dinner at the Waldorf Hotel. Landis, advised of the settlement, dismissed the antitrust suit.

Major-league teams bought out owners in cities where the Federal League had established clubs in competition with major-league franchises. Some Federal League owners, such as Charles Weeghman of Chicago, were offered the opportunity to purchase interests in existing clubs, and they were quickly transformed from villains into fellow sportsmen. The magnates offered Ned Hanlon, owner of the Federal League Baltimore Terrapins, a pittance as settlement because the major leagues did not have a franchise in Baltimore. To add insult to financial injury, one magnate attacked Baltimore as a "minor league city, and not a hell of a good one at that." Needless to say, Hanlon turned down the offer.

Admitted to the Hall of Fame in 1996, Ned Hanlon spent his life in the game of baseball, first from 1880 until 1892 as a player (and an active Brotherhood member) and then for nineteen years as the successful manager of the Baltimore, Brooklyn, and Cincinnati franchises. Hanlon felt cheated and insulted by the major-league owners' slights. His Federal Baseball Club of Baltimore, Inc., brought an antitrust suit in federal court in the District of Columbia (then called the Supreme Court of the District) against American and National League owners and three of the Federal League owners whom they had favored with larger offers. The complaint alleged that a conspiracy among the defendants, in violation of the antitrust laws, had resulted in damage to Hanlon's business.

Hanlon alleged that the major leagues had successfully sought to "wreck and destroy" the Federal League. He complained of major-league baseball's "oppressive, intimidating, and coercive course of conduct" and "despotic control." His complaint stressed the "humiliation" to the citizens of Baltimore, which "tended to lessen its [the city's] standing and prestige." Hanlon also alleged that the players who might have accepted employment in the Federal League were bound by a "system of peonage," enforced by threats of a perpetual blacklist. Finally, he argued that the major leagues broke the Federal League through "transactions which amount to nothing less than bribery" that had induced owners "to betray and desert the other clubs." The total cost to the major leagues to buy off their rivals, according to Hanlon, was $750,000. (Actually, it was closer to $5 million.) No other case, he said, ever showed "such an example of ruthless conduct toward a competitor, or of shameless disregard of his fundamental property rights."

After a three-week trial in 1919, the jury awarded Hanlon $80,000, trebled by Judge Wendell P. Stafford under the provisions of the antitrust statute. On appeal to the United States Court of Appeals for the District of Columbia, major-league baseball's attorney, George Wharton Pepper, argued that the antitrust laws did not cover the sport. Baseball, he wrote, was "a spontaneous output of human activity . . . not in its nature commerce." The court of appeals agreed, ruling: "The fact that the [club owners] produce baseball games as a source of profit, large or small, cannot change the character of the games. They are still sport, not trade." Moreover, the game was "local in its beginning and in its end." Hanlon then brought his claim to the United States Supreme Court.

On April 19, 1922, the day before the baseball season began in the District of Columbia, the Supreme Court heard oral argument in the *Federal Baseball* case. Chief Justice William Howard Taft, former president of the United States, a great lover of the game, and a third baseman at Yale, presided. In 1912, President Taft had initiated the custom of the president throwing out the first ball on Opening Day. Taft is also credited with originating the "seventh-inning stretch" when, during a 1910 Pittsburgh Pirates game, he rose midway through the seventh inning to stretch his abundant torso; the entire crowd stood up out of respect. It is also reported that Taft had been offered the newly created position of baseball commissioner, which he declined. Despite this history, Taft apparently did not feel it necessary to recuse himself from participating in this landmark baseball court case because of a conflict of interest.

Pepper argued the case for the American, National, and Federal League owners before the Supreme Court. He suggested that "the very existence of baseball depended upon its exemption from the antitrust laws." The national pastime was at stake, and the Court must not let down the nation.

The Court issued its decision about a month later, on May 29. Justice Oliver Wendell Holmes, writing for a unanimous Court, affirmed the appellate court's decision denying Hanlon's claim. He offered a "summary statement of the nature of the business" of baseball:

> The clubs composing the Leagues are in different cities for the most part in different States. . . . These clubs . . . play against one another in public exhibitions for money, one or the other club crossing a state line in order to make the meeting possible. When as the result of these contests one club has won the pennant

of its League and another club has won the pennant of the other League, there is a final competition for the world's championship between these two. Of course, the scheme requires constantly repeated travelling on the part of the clubs, which is provided for, controlled and disciplined by the organizations, and this is said means commerce among the States.

Holmes concluded, however, that baseball exhibitions, although a business, were "purely state affairs." They did not constitute interstate commerce, as covered by the antitrust laws. Traveling across state lines to stage these exhibitions was "a mere incident, not the essential thing." Baseball, the exhibition, was not even "commerce" because "personal effort, not related to production, is not a subject of commerce." Therefore, Congress never intended the antitrust laws to cover baseball. Decades later, a critical federal appellate court would comment that May 29, 1922, the day the Supreme Court issued the opinion, was "not one of Mr. Justice Holmes' happiest days." It was, of course, one of organized baseball's happiest days.

Analysis of *Federal Baseball*

Federal Baseball, a watershed decision, established an antitrust exemption for professional baseball. The opinion has since been criticized as ludicrous, but perhaps it reflects the then-current notions of interstate commerce. Although by the 1920s baseball had become a major business, Holmes's legal analysis must be appraised in the jurisprudential context of the time.

The antitrust statute that the *Federal Baseball* Court interpreted required proof that the defendant was involved in "interstate commerce" before the prohibitions against collusion applied. The Commerce Clause of the Constitution gave Congress the power to legislate against the abuses of business combinations that affected *inter*state, but not *intra*state, commerce. Without the "nexus" to interstate commerce, Congress had no power to legislate. Therefore, the Supreme Court was certainly correct to focus on this issue.

The relationship between the legislative and judicial branches of government requires a delicate balancing of their institutional prerogatives. When Congress acts within its constitutional power, its choices from among various regulatory schemes must control court decision making. The *Federal Baseball* Court did not question the constitutionality of the antitrust laws, only their reach to the business of baseball. Congress's intent would be the controlling factor, as it is in any case involving statutory interpretation. How should the Court determine what Congress wanted?

One way a court determines legislative intent is to examine a statute's history within the legislative process. When the members of a legislature vote on a proposed law, they generally have available written committee reports and transcripts of hearings. Normally, the legislative body records its own debate on legislation. These sources may inform a court about what the legislature sought to halt or promote and about what entities the legislature wanted to regulate.

The legislative history of the antitrust laws—the Sherman Antitrust Act in 1890 and the Clayton Antitrust Act in 1914—is thin. Congress was concerned with the growing power of monopolies, particularly those that eliminated competition in industrial America. There is no evidence that any member of Congress even thought about the baseball enterprise. If there was a special antitrust exemption for baseball, it was one the Supreme Court would have to divine from the words of the statutes, because Congress never considered the question.

The antitrust statutes, however, did require proof of a business's effect on interstate commerce in order to find the proscriptions applicable. Interpreting this provision, courts had ruled that Congress intended to reach manufacturers of products that used raw materials transported across state lines or that distributed finished goods across state lines. Under prevailing court rulings, the antitrust laws did not cover purely intrastate manufacturers. But baseball did not involve the production of goods at all. Should not that alone be sufficient to justify Holmes's conclusion?

Even by the early 1920s, the concept of "commerce" had grown beyond simple manufacturing. A case heard the next Supreme Court term raises serious questions about the soundness of *Federal Baseball.* Holmes again wrote for a unanimous Supreme Court, in a case involving the application of the antitrust laws to a traveling vaudeville show. This time he reasoned that the transport of the vaudeville show "apparatus" in interstate commerce might be sufficient to trigger statutory coverage. Apparently, moving sets and costumes across state lines triggered the antitrust regulations, but moving uniforms, bats, and balls did not. The only way the two cases can be reconciled is by concluding that one involved baseball and the other involved vaudeville. But both baseball and vaudeville are show business.

What, then, explains *Federal Baseball?* Could the Supreme Court have shown such solicitude for this business because the enterprise in question was the national pastime? The attorney for the major leagues made that very argument before the Supreme Court, although even in 1922 that justification had no basis in the law. Baseball does have an effect on rational judgment, however, as we shall see in Curt Flood's case.

Almost a quarter century after the *Federal Baseball* decision, M. Lindsey Cowen, then a student editor of the *Virginia Law Review* (later dean of the law schools at the University of Georgia and Case Western Reserve University), wrote approvingly of the *Federal Baseball* precedent: although "legal theorists" and "labor executives may deplore the situation . . . so long as the governance of Baseball is benevolent and the public receives the quality of sport it wants, there is no compelling reason to alter the situation." When Cowen wrote this commentary, Landis had "benevolently" governed baseball for almost a quarter century, and the sport was more popular than ever.

The Toolson Litigation

Thirty years after *Federal Baseball,* in 1953, the Supreme Court had another opportunity to address the reach of the antitrust laws in *Toolson v. New York Yankees.* George Toolson was a minor leaguer with the Yankees' franchise team, the Newark Bears. When the Yankees reassigned him to another club, Toolson refused to report and filed suit. He claimed that management's order under the reserve system violated the antitrust laws. Based on the *Federal Baseball* precedent, however, the lower courts dismissed Toolson's challenge.

During the years between *Federal Baseball* and *Toolson,* the Supreme Court had repeatedly distinguished its 1922 precedent in cases involving exhibitions and entertainments that crossed state lines, and, in the process, it had expanded the concept of interstate commerce. In addition, by 1953 there could be no question that the baseball enterprise was a business inextricably entwined with interstate commerce. Baseball games were now broadcast on radio and television across the country. Indeed, in *Toolson* the dissenting opinion filed by Justice Harold Burton and joined by Justice Stanley Reed recognized that the *Federal Baseball* precedent had lost its factual and legal

basis. Burton wrote that organized baseball obviously was engaged in interstate trade or commerce. The majority of the Supreme Court, however, in a
one-paragraph *per curiam* decision not signed by any individual justice, reaffirmed the *Federal Baseball* ruling:

> Congress has had the [*Federal Baseball*] ruling under consideration but has not
> seen fit to bring such business under these laws by legislation. . . . The business
> has thus been left for thirty years to develop, on the understanding that it was
> not subject to existing antitrust legislation. The present cases ask us to overrule
> the prior decision. . . . We think that if there are evils in this field which now war-
> rant application to it of the antitrust laws, it should be by legislation.

The Court made it clear: if change was to come, it was up to Congress to make
it happen.

Congressional Inaction

The Supreme Court correctly stated in *Toolson* that Congress had been given
the opportunity to address *Federal Baseball*—either to affirm it or to overrule it through new legislation. In 1951, Congress considered four bills (three
in the House, one in the Senate) that would have *continued* baseball's antitrust exemption, but it enacted none of them. The House Subcommittee on
the Study of Monopoly Power, chaired by Congressman Emanuel Cellars of
New York, took testimony from industry witnesses, including dozens of baseball players, and only one, renegade owner Bill Veeck, criticized the reserve
system. Cellars later explained that his committee was plagued by incessant
lobbying: "I want to say . . . that I have never known, in my 35 years of experience, of as great a lobby that descended upon the House than the organized
baseball lobby. . . . They came upon Washington like locusts."

The subcommittee recognized the economic impact of the reserve system,
but it issued a report in 1952 recommending that Congress postpone further
consideration of pending legislation until the Supreme Court decided the
Toolson case: "The subcommittee recognizes . . . that baseball is a unique industry. . . . The history of baseball has demonstrated that cooperation in many
of the details of the operation of the baseball business is essential to the maintenance of honest and vigorous competition on the playing field." The sub-

committee further stated there was no need to enact a special rule exempting the reserve clause from the antitrust laws:

> Organized baseball, represented by eminent counsel, has assured this subcom-
> mittee that the legality of the reserve clause will be tested by the [antitrust law's]
> rule of reason. . . . It would therefore seem premature to enact general legisla-
> tion for baseball at this time. Legislation is not necessary until the reasonable-
> ness of the reserve rules has been tested by the courts.

Congress thus refused to act based on the pledge by baseball's attorney that
the courts would review the reserve system under the antitrust laws. Later,
in the *Toolson* case, counsel for the major leagues argued that the Supreme
Court should not reach the merits of the antitrust claim, because Holmes had
ruled the antitrust laws were not applicable to baseball. The Supreme Court
played along with this legislative pepper game and sidestepped the antitrust
challenge in *Toolson,* saying it was up to Congress and not the Supreme Court
to change the law.

While one could argue that *Federal Baseball* reflected the prevailing limited conception of interstate commerce, the Supreme Court's action in *Toolson* is indefensible. By the time the Court issued its abbreviated anonymous
opinion, Congress had completed a comprehensive review of the baseball industry. It did not adopt the pending legislation that would have embodied the
Federal Baseball rule in federal statutory law. The report of the congressional
subcommittee recommended against action because the Supreme Court had
the issue before it and anticipated, with good reason, that the Court would
apply the antitrust laws. Remarkably, the Supreme Court then read this legislative inaction as a ratification of *Federal Baseball.*

Congress's failure or refusal to act is perfectly understandable. Baseball
was too hot an issue to address, and members of Congress had to respect the
owners' political clout. Although Congress may be excused for reacting in a
political manner—it is, after all, supposed to respond to political forces—
nothing can excuse the Supreme Court's timidity or the duplicity of baseball
counsel in misleading Congress.

In his dissent in *Toolson,* Justice Burton read Congress's failure to act quite
differently than did the majority: Congress had shown that it knew how ex-
pressly to exempt certain activities from the antitrust laws, as it had done with
labor organizations, farm cooperatives, and the insurance business. Thus, said

Burton, Congress's failure to exempt baseball, although it had been repeatedly pressed to do so, must mean that no exemption was intended. Justice Burton's argument persuaded only Justice Reed on the nine-member Supreme Court.

Stare Decisis and the Conservative Judiciary

Some political leaders perennially criticize courts as activist engines of social change. To the contrary, stability is the prevailing judicial ethos. Courts essentially are conservative institutions. Private decisions, far more dramatically than the judiciary, drive society in one direction or another. As we will see, for example, it was Branch Rickey and the economics of baseball, not a judicial fiat, that led to the desegregation of the major leagues in 1947.

The fundamental tenet of judicial decision making is that "like cases should be decided alike." Of course, what constitutes a "like case" is not always obvious. Therein lies the hard work of judging. Courts maintain the stability and legitimacy of the judicial process through the reasoned analysis of abstract characteristics and the consistent application of a body of principles. Circumstances may warrant rethinking earlier principles, but for the most part, prior law controls future cases—a principle called *stare decisis*.

Effective private social ordering requires stability of principle and predictability of judicial results. Judicial conservatism facilitates primary private activity and allows people to plan. Otherwise, private parties could not predict whether courts would enforce the bargains they reach. By custom and tradition, courts find controlling and authoritative those principles used by courts in the past to resolve similar disputes. Courts from one state may even look to decisions from another state for guidance, although they are not compelled to follow rulings from another jurisdiction.

The practice of adhering to prior principles generally is efficient and fair. Without it, in each case the parties would have to start from scratch, relitigating the fundamental core instead of the margins of controlling principles. Most disputes actually arise where principles overlap. The men and women who constitute our judicial officers change over time, and if precedent did not have any restraining effect, the appointment of a new judge to the court would herald an effort to rewrite the "black letter"—or long-standing, well-established—law.

Predictability of result flows from judicial adherence to precedent. This, in turn, engenders public confidence in the stability of the law, divorced, as it must be, from subjective reevaluation by each new set of judges. If judges were totally unbound by precedent, tradition, custom, and political accountability, what would restrain them from reshaping prior holdings based on personal preferences?

Judicial precedent, however, can go only so far. The needs of society change over time, and the common law must be renewed and revitalized. We depend not only on the stability of rules but also on the flexibility of principle to react to the dynamic conditions of modern life. Precedent is reinterpreted, narrowed, or stretched to accommodate changing circumstances. At times, a precedent is recognized as ill conceived and unsound. In such cases, courts overrule decisions and set the law on the correct course.

Of course, this traditional analysis of judicial decision making presents an idealized model. Beginning with the Realist movement of the 1920s, legal commentators have recognized the central importance of the views of individual judges within the legal process. More recently, advocates of the Critical Legal Studies movement have focused on the indeterminacy of language and the overriding importance of politics in judicial decision making. These powerful intellectual currents have fostered a well-grounded skepticism in the ostensibly objective nature of judicial reasoning. They present variations from the traditional theme that make the judicial process more human than disinterested, more irrational than coherent.

Society operates within a mythology of judicial objectivism, however, which lends legitimacy to the legal process. Although these rival ideologies present persuasive arguments, we can also test prevailing court-made law on the grounds judges purport to follow. As often as not, as we have seen with the *Toolson* case, judicial opinions fail on those grounds, without need to resort to alternate visions of jurisprudence.

The Flood Litigation

In 1972, Curt Flood offered the Supreme Court one last opportunity to bring baseball precedent in line with the prevailing antitrust law. Flood had been a strong performer for over a decade in the St. Louis outfield, with a .293 lifetime batting average and a .987 fielding percentage. He once played 226 games in a row without making an error. After a strong season in 1968, he asked Cardinals' owner August "Gussie" Busch for a $30,000 raise. Busch was incensed; he denied the request and privately vowed retribution. On October 7, 1969, Flood received a telephone call from a minion in the Cardinals' front office, informing him he had been traded. The Cardinals had sent Flood, Tim McCarver, Joe Hoerner, and Byron Browne to Philadelphia in exchange for Dick Allen, Octavio "Cookie" Rojas, and Jerry Johnson.

Curt Flood refused to report to the Phillies. At age thirty-one, he did not want to move his family again, leave his business interests in St. Louis, and finish his career playing before Philadelphia crowds that were known for being hard on black players. Flood wrote to Commissioner Bowie Kuhn: "After 12 years in the Major Leagues, I do not feel I am a piece of property to be bought and sold irrespective of my wishes. I believe that any system which produces that result violates my basic rights as a citizen." Kuhn responded that if Flood did not agree to play for the Philadelphia club, he could choose not to play professional baseball.

With the financial support of the Major League Baseball Players Association, Flood fought back. Represented in federal court by former Supreme Court justice Arthur Goldberg, Flood filed suit in New York City. Observers report that Goldberg, who had been selected by the Players Association, was an embarrassing choice. In the end, he lost a case that a more skilled advocate might have won. Both the trial court and the United States Court of Appeals for the Second Circuit dismissed Flood's action based on the *Federal Baseball* and *Toolson* precedent, not a surprising outcome. District court judge Irving Ben Cooper, foreshadowing Flood's treatment before the nation's highest court, wrote:

> To put it mildly and with restraint, it would be unfortunate indeed if a fine sport and profession, which brings surcease from daily travail and as escape from the ordinary to most inhabitants of this land, were to suffer in the least because of undue concentration by any one or any group on commercial and profit consideration. The game is on higher ground; it behooves every one to keep it there.

The Second Circuit Court of Appeals felt "compelled to affirm" Cooper's decision. Then the Supreme Court granted Flood's petition for certiorari, "in order to look once again at this troublesome and unusual situation." It heard oral argument on the matter on March 20, 1972.

After the oral argument, Chief Justice Warren Burger assigned the writing of the opinion to his old friend, fellow Minnesotan Justice Harry Blackmun. Blackmun was a devoted baseball fan. His opinion for a majority of the court, issued less than three months later, upheld the judgment of the lower courts and reaffirmed the tainted line of baseball cases. The opinion is an unprecedented combination of sentimentalism and awkward judicial formalism, an embarrassment for a justice who would later earn a deserved reputation as a truly distinguished jurist.

Blackmun began his majority opinion in *Flood v. Kuhn* with an anthem of praise for baseball mythology, listing his personal choices for the players who "have sparked the diamond and its environs and . . . have provided tinder for recaptured thrills, for reminiscence and comparisons and for conversation and anticipation in-season and off-season." It is reported that, after he circulated this draft to other Justices, Justice Thurgood Marshall telephoned Blackmun to complain that there were no black ballplayers on his list of great players. Blackmun, clearly concerned, told Marshall that there were no black players during the golden age of baseball; Marshall responded that this was exactly his point. Blackmun thereafter added black players to his roster— Jackie Robinson, Leroy "Satchel" Paige, and Roy Campanella—but Marshall never had any intention of joining the majority. He dissented, writing a stinging decision that revealed the flaws of Blackmun's entire approach to the issue of precedent. Blackmun's introductory section was so offensive to Justice Byron White that while he joined in the decision, he disassociated himself from Blackmun's opening paean to the national pastime.

Once past his flowery commencement, which included references to the highlights of a century of organized ball and the poem "Casey at the Bat," Blackmun set about the tedious chore of reviewing every Supreme Court antitrust decision after *Federal Baseball* that addressed the question of the reach of the statute's interstate commerce language. Blackmun's conscientious case-after-case analysis proved that the baseball exemption, beyond any doubt, was an aberration. As noted above, the year after *Federal Baseball* the Supreme Court ruled the transportation of actors and equipment across state lines to be interstate commerce. The Supreme Court then held that professional boxing and football were covered by the antitrust laws. By the time of

Flood's case, the statutes covered every professional sports enterprise, with one exception: organized baseball.

Later in his opinion, Blackmun bluntly and clearly repudiated the holding in *Federal Baseball*, stating that professional baseball is a business involved in interstate commerce and that baseball's special status is an "anomaly." Congress's failure to act to exempt baseball (what Blackmun termed "positive inaction," an interesting concept) was once again offered as a justification for judicial inaction. Under Blackmun's theory, Congress legislates by not legislating.

Justice Blackmun concluded that the strange *Federal Baseball* precedent had been around so long as to be unchangeable by the Supreme Court that created it. It was an established aberration, "entitled to the benefits of *stare decisis*." There is "merit in consistency even though some might claim that beneath that consistency is a layer of inconsistency." Ultimately, *Federal Baseball* survived and Flood lost.

Marshall's dissent skillfully dissected the majority opinion—admittedly, not a very difficult task. The Supreme Court had regularly overruled precedent it determined to be in error but would not do so here, despite the majority's clear statement that the precedent was wrong. It made no sense to leave baseball outside the reach of federal law when basketball, football, and hockey were covered. Reflecting on Flood's central concern, Marshall reasoned that the "virtual slavery" of the reserve system should not be allowed to stand. Congress had never acquiesced to this "abomination." Since it was the Court that had made baseball players impotent and isolated, Marshall reasoned that the Court should correct its error.

Considered as a whole, Blackmun's majority opinion may have confused the *business* of baseball with the glorious *game* of baseball, the national pastime wrapped in legend and myth that began with the Cooperstown saga. The baseball enterprise is, after all, just another commercial amusement for which people pay money, bound in all other ways by the laws that apply to all other private parties in society. Baseball clubs and owners are not immune from criminal laws, zoning ordinances, and health regulations; but under Supreme Court precedent, these sportsmen are immune from the antitrust laws. After Curt Flood's failed challenge, it was apparent that the courts would never apply the antitrust laws to invalidate baseball's reserve system. The baseball cartel would be able to maintain its monopsony, controlling player salaries without judicial interference.

Perhaps the Supreme Court's refusal to overrule *Federal Baseball* can be justified according to the different competencies of governmental institutions. Courts and legislatures have discrete capabilities and limitations. A court decides the cases brought before it, relying, for the most part, on the arguments made by the disputing parties, the facts in the record, and existing precedent. With rare exceptions, an American court may not seek out evidence on its own. It depends on the adversarial system to uncover and present the facts to the tribunal. (By comparison, many European countries approach judicial fact-finding differently. For example, in Germany a trial judge is expected to bring out all the "objective facts." A German judge is often an "aggressive inquisitor," not simply a passive player in the judicial process.) Legislatures, in contrast, can investigate, hold hearings, find "facts," and then act.

A court is limited in the range of remedies it may consider to redress a wrong. A legislature, however, may carefully tailor solutions to address a particular problem. It need not wait until someone brings it a problem but may venture forth on its own initiative. Legislatures enjoy vast discretion, bounded only by politics, majority rule, custom, and the Constitution.

Compared to the courts, Congress could do a much better job fine-tuning the application of the antitrust laws to baseball's reserve system. Under its power to regulate interstate commerce, Congress could condition baseball's continued exemption with legislation that might limit the reserve system to a certain number of players for a fixed time period. The Court, ruling on the merits of Curt Flood's claim, had very limited choices: it could find the antitrust laws applicable or inapplicable, violated or not violated. It could not redesign the reserve system.

There are two problems with this "legislatures can do it better" justification for the *Flood* decision. The legislative branch always has the power to use the scalpel instead of the sledgehammer. But does this mean courts should always refrain from overruling their own misguided or outmoded precedent? Furthermore, by the time the Supreme Court issued *Flood*, it was apparent that Congress could not, or would not, act on this volatile and highly politicized issue. General notions of institutional capabilities were rebutted in this context. Congress could not act; the Supreme Court could, but chose not to.

In appraising *Flood*, we must recognize that the Supreme Court had boxed itself in by the reasoning in prior cases. In every case after *Federal Baseball*, the Court took pains to distinguish this precedent from the matter at hand. Were these distinctions no longer valid? Had the Court been wrong not only in *Federal Baseball* but in a long line of cases that explained the progenitor decision?

In *Toolson* the Court ruled that the baseball industry had relied on the *Federal Baseball* immunity. If the Supreme Court in *Flood* was going to overrule these precedents, it would have to conclude either that the baseball club owners did not rely on the immunity or that the reliance interest was not as important as correcting the law. We know that, after *Federal Baseball*, the business leaders of baseball did nothing on their own to modify the reserve system. Does that constitute proof of reliance?

Flood stands as a notable example of judicial powerlessness in the face of a self-created dilemma, an object lesson in conservative principles run amok, and a textbook example of the limits of the reform power of public institutions. The Supreme Court should not bear the entire blame. Congress had many opportunities to alter the course of baseball's antitrust exemption or to reaffirm its correctness, but it sat quietly in the dugout.

Although Curt Flood struck out, his efforts were significant. By fighting the reserve system, Flood showed that he would not compromise his principles or his dignity. At the time of his death from throat cancer in 1997, Flood was recognized universally as a champion of the players revolution. His failed lawsuit proved to the ballplayers and their union that Monte Ward had been correct many decades earlier: if the players were going to improve their lot, it would have to be through collective action, economic strength, and private dispute resolution, not through traditional court litigation based on public laws. Within the decade, these union-based strategies would tally winning scores for the players. Under the collective bargaining regime, players would stay out of court and use alternative dispute-resolution methods of negotiation and arbitration to seek redress for what they perceived as the power imbalance in the business of baseball.

The *Federal Baseball, Toolson,* and *Flood* trilogy is a remarkable example of the Supreme Court's incapacity to address legal issues arising out of the national pastime. Whatever the merits of the individual decisions, the Supreme Court cannot be proud of an outcome so many have found inexplicable and indefensible.

4: Collective Bargaining

MARVIN MILLER

Marvin Miller, the dapper economist from Brooklyn, converted a social fraternity of baseball players into the strongest trade union in America. Under his leadership, for the first time in a century of organized baseball, the players received a significant share of the profits of the baseball enterprise. In the process, however, the game would be interrupted by periodic work stoppages and employer lockouts. *(Photo courtesy of Corbis-Bettmann and National Baseball Hall of Fame Library, Cooperstown, N.Y.)*

The unionization of professional athletes has been the most

important labor relations development in professional sports since their inception. Once again, baseball took the lead. The Major League Baseball Players Association transformed the baseball enterprise through astute negotiations, triumphant arbitrations, and the use of periodic work stoppages, all made possible by a solidarity among the players that astonished the club owners.

Started as a fraternal organization of ballplayers in the early 1950s, the Players Association became one of the nation's most powerful trade unions. For this development, one man deserves the credit: the starting "union leader" on our All-Star Baseball Law Team roster, Marvin Miller. His able successor, Executive Director Donald Fehr, has demonstrated similar stalwart traits, coming off the bench to continue the association's winning streak.

The Players Association was the fifth labor organization of baseball players, but it was the first to achieve significant success in dealing with club owners. The first union, the Brotherhood of the 1880s, disappeared in the ashes of the Players League. The League Protective Players' Association lasted two seasons, from 1900 to 1902, during the American League's war with the National League. Attorney David Fultz started the Baseball Players' Fraternity in 1912, and it lasted through the Federal League era until 1918. Lawyer Robert Murphy led the fourth union, the American Baseball Guild, for one season in 1946. The difference between the achievements of Miller's Major League Baseball Players Association and the ephemeral impact of its predecessors is dramatic: this union not only has endured but has revolutionized the labor relations of the sport.

For years, the Players Association was anything but a real union. In fact, payments from the owners financed Players Association activities, a patent violation of the National Labor Relations Act. Miller's predecessor, Judge Robert Cannon, steadfastly supported the owners' reserve system and testified before Congress in 1964, "We have it so good we don't know what to ask for next." And when the leaders of the Players Association—Robin Roberts, Jim Bunning, Bob Friend, and Harvey Kuenn—established a search committee to select a new full-time spokesman for the players in 1965, there was no indication that they were dissatisfied with their organization's direction. Roberts sought advice from Wharton School of Business professor George Taylor, a leading labor economist, who suggested Marvin James Miller, the chief economist with the Steelworkers Union for the previous sixteen years. A Brooklyn Dodgers fan by birth, Miller, a dapper unionist with a pencil-thin mustache, was intrigued by the challenge, although it was clear to him that the major-league baseball players had no concept of true trade unionism.

In 1966, association leaders offered Miller the position and he accepted; but he conditioned his assent on membership approval. Miller knew he needed the support of rank-and-file players if he was going to transform the association into an effective labor organization that would win a greater share of the game's profits for the players. He toured the spring training camps, listening to players' concerns about pensions and ill treatment from the club owners. Miller won approval by a vote of 489–136.

When Miller took over as executive director, the union owned a file cabinet and had $5,400 in its bank account. He immediately negotiated a deal with Coca-Cola to put players' pictures under bottle caps, raising $66,000—the modest beginning of a licensing program that subsequently would produce millions of dollars in revenue for baseball players.

Miller established the first permanent office for the union on Park Avenue in New York City and hired Richard M. Moss as legal counsel. (The players had strongly recommended to Miller that he select former vice president Richard M. Nixon as his general counsel, advice displaying the naivete of the union leadership.) The choice of Dick Moss was a brilliant stroke. Moss worked at Miller's side to transform the Players Association into a real trade union.

National Labor Policy

Until the passage of the Wagner Act in 1935, federal labor policy discouraged employee unionization. Unprotected by federal law and subject to injunction suits in federal and state courts, labor unions struggled to exist in the face of unyielding employer opposition. In fact, during the mid-nineteenth century, unions were considered criminal conspiracies in many states, and their leaders were subject to arrest. Companies hired and fired workers at will, unilaterally imposing terms of employment that reflected the disparate bargaining power between workers and employers.

National labor policy changed dramatically as a result of the Great Depression. In the Norris-LaGuardia Act of 1930, Congress removed the threat of a federal court injunction against peaceful union strikes. Then, in the Wagner Act of 1935, Congress affirmatively supported the right of employees to organize unions, to engage in peaceful concerted activities, and to demand that employers bargain in good faith with organizations representing a majority of their employees. Unions could now argue with some justification that the government wanted employees to form unions. Although it did not mandate the results of collective bargaining, Congress made the economic prediction that through unionization, employees would increase their bargaining power and, in turn, elevate wages decreased by the Great Depression's economic calamity.

The Wagner Act is a good example of the role of government as a facilitator of private interaction, rather than as a manager of the details of societal ordering. Congress did not set wages beyond a basic minimum level. Instead, Congress borrowed as its model the existing practice in a few industries; the terms and conditions of employment would be set by private, and not public, regulation. As long as Congress's legislative framework was clear, labor and management could adjust their differences privately without governmental intervention, except in rare cases. The Wagner Act proposed that labor conflicts be settled by the disputing parties themselves through the structure of collective bargaining.

Congress also knew that not all disputes would be resolved simply by the legislative branch passing a statute that declared the rights of employees and unions. In typical New Deal fashion, it created a special tribunal to enforce the Wagner Act's commands. An administrative agency, the National Labor Relations Board, would protect rights created by the legislation and declare certain employer conduct "unfair labor practices," which could then be remedied through court-enforced orders and damages.

Unlike the European model, where national legislatures enact into law agreements reached on an industry-wide level by employer and union representatives, the American model provides for decentralized decision making regarding terms and conditions of employment, with little legislative or administrative oversight. The processes of collective bargaining result in stable terms of employment that reflect the relative power of the parties involved in the negotiations, rather than a solution imposed by government. Strong unions win good deals; weak unions suffer at the bargaining table. That was Congress's intention.

The Wagner Act, later balanced by the pro-employer Taft-Hartley Amendments and fine-tuned by the Landrum-Griffin Act, formed the remarkably durable National Labor Relations Act, the heart of national labor policy, which has remained fundamentally unchanged for more than half a century. Under national labor policy, private choice, not government fiat, controls. Employees can organize unions or decline to do so, but majority vote rules. Companies cannot interfere with employee free choice by discriminating against those who have favored or opposed a union. The law also limits union tactics; for example, unions cannot pressure employers for concessions by entangling neutral customers or suppliers in their labor disputes. The National Labor Relations Board, a comparatively small federal agency that has exercised its powers judiciously, umpires any disputes that allege violations of federal labor law.

Congress enacted this labor legislation under its constitutional power to regulate commerce between the states. Therefore, the statute could cover only employers involved in interstate commerce. The National Labor Relations Board would not protect the organizational and bargaining efforts of those who worked for employers not covered by the National Labor Relations Act. For most employers and employees, the interstate commerce requirement was a small hurdle; under expansive interpretations of the Interstate Commerce Clause, the Supreme Court had upheld far-reaching New Deal legislation. For professional baseball players, however, the interstate commerce barrier seemed insurmountable.

In the *Federal Baseball* decision (discussed in Chapter 3), Justice Oliver Wendell Holmes had ruled that the business of baseball did not affect interstate commerce. Later reaffirmed in *Toolson* and *Flood,* the prevailing law appeared to doom Players Association recourse to federal protections in its battles with baseball management. Aid for the players' seemingly hopeless cause came from a most unlikely source—baseball's umpires.

Labor Board Jurisdiction

During the late 1960s, the American League's umpires sought to organize a union to bargain collectively with the league over the terms and conditions of their employment. The umpires turned to the National Labor Relations Board for assistance. In addition to its role in enforcing rights protected by statute through its unfair labor practice proceedings, the Labor Board has the power to conduct secret-ballot elections to determine if a majority of employees want to be represented by a union for purposes of collective bargaining. To obtain an election order, a union has to submit evidence to the Labor Board that at least 30 percent of the employees in the election unit (called the "appropriate bargaining unit") support unionization. Unions normally make this "showing of interest" by presenting the agency with authorization cards signed by employees.

The umpires' union filed a petition with the Labor Board in 1969, requesting that it conduct an election among American League umpires. The league objected, claiming that baseball did not affect interstate commerce under the antitrust exemption cases. The umpires also faced unfavorable Labor Board precedent: the agency had earlier declined jurisdiction over the horse-racing industry, concluding it was a "local activity" beyond the board's purview. Did the National Labor Relations Act cover the business of baseball?

In what must be considered one of the greatest upsets in the history of baseball and the legal process, a four-to-one majority of the Labor Board ruled that it would take jurisdiction over the major-league baseball enterprise. The agency spurned the *Federal Baseball* precedent as an aged artifact. In 1969, three years before the Supreme Court would once again reaffirm *Federal Baseball* in the *Flood* decision, the Labor Board concluded that the Supreme Court had effectively overruled earlier precedent through the series of cases that had held that all other professional team sports affected interstate commerce. Obviously, said the Labor Board, baseball *did* affect interstate commerce.

In its presentation to the Labor Board, the league cited the horse racing precedent and argued that even if baseball affected interstate commerce, the agency should exercise its discretion to decline to take jurisdiction. The sport's impact on interstate commerce was insubstantial, according to the league. However, the evidence before the Labor Board belied the owners' argument. Millions of dollars of goods and services flowed across state lines in support of the baseball industry. Moreover, the horse-racing case was not persuasive. Unlike baseball, horse racing is subject to close state supervision because of its open gambling.

The American League also argued that there was no need for agency intervention in baseball because the industry already had an internal self-regulatory mechanism—the commissioner's office. The Labor Board should not waste its valuable time, the league argued, because the commissioner would keep any labor dispute from having a substantial impact on interstate commerce. Rejecting this supposition, the Labor Board pointed out that because the commissioner was selected and paid by the owners, he was not a neutral party, and consequently, he was unlikely to prevent labor disputes or resolve them. In any case, it would violate national labor policy to defer board jurisdiction to a dispute-settlement system established unilaterally by an employer. Congress's labor legislation envisioned a neutral arbiter, the Labor Board, not one handpicked and paid by one party.

In a creative parting argument, the league contended that the umpires were supervisors and that, under Section 2(11) of the National Labor Relations Act, Congress excluded "supervisors" from statutory coverage. The law listed "disciplining" and "directing" employees as supervisory functions. Didn't the umpires "discipline" players by tossing them out of the contest? Didn't the home plate umpire "order" the player to take his base upon receipt of four balls or being hit by a thrown pitch? The Labor Board was not confused by this sophistry; obviously, umpires just enforced the rules of the game, which were established by the owners. In this regard, umpires were analogous to plant guards, who were employees covered by the Labor Act.

In a lone dissent written by Labor Board member Howard Jenkins, who normally favored employee organizational rights, the mythology of baseball overtook legal reasoning. Jenkins foreshadowed Blackmun's opinion in *Flood* when he wrote of baseball's unique and favored place in the "heart and minds" of the American people. Jenkins stated that he could find no evidence that the baseball industry would be racked by labor disputes. He was a poor prognosticator.

The Labor Board took jurisdiction over the baseball industry, and the American League umpires voted in a secret election, supervised by Labor Board employees. A majority of the umpires voted for the union, and the agency "certified" the union as the exclusive bargaining representative for all the American League umpires. The certification was later expanded to cover all baseball umpires at the major-league level.

The Practice of Collective Bargaining

Labor Board certification does not mean that employees receive automatic raises or even that they obtain a contract with their employer. It only gives a union "a license to fish" in the waters of collective bargaining. Under the terms of the National Labor Relations Act, management and labor are required to meet and negotiate over "terms and conditions of employment." Neither side is required to make concessions, but both must bargain "in good faith" by making a reasonable effort to agree on contract terms. A claim that the opposing party (normally management) has failed to bargain in good faith, as required by law, can be brought before the Labor Board by filing an unfair labor practice charge.

"Good faith" bargaining is a difficult concept to explain. It is measured by a party's conduct within the negotiation process. Some actions, such as delaying scheduled meetings or refusing reasonable requests for information, show that an employer is not willing to negotiate with an open mind and a sincere desire to find a basis for agreement. Each side must be willing to meet and discuss its demands. Even though it need not make any concessions, management cannot simply stonewall on union proposals. Management does not have to accept union demands, but it does have to engage in the negotiation process.

The statutory duty to bargain in good faith is designed to facilitate, but not mandate, agreement. Collective bargaining is an example of purely "autonomous ordering." National labor policy provides the structure within which labor and management can reach agreement over terms and conditions of employment through collective bargaining. The terms of the contract—the legislation of this "private government"—then regulate the workplace for the duration of the agreement.

Management must supply the union, upon request, with information that might be relevant to the bargaining process. The information must be made available with reasonable promptness and in a form the union can use. A parity of information at the negotiating table enhances the quality of negotiations and encourages creativity and flexibility in reaching a settlement. The certified union has a statutory obligation to "fairly represent" all of its members, and the information management supplies about current terms and conditions of employment will assist the union in meeting this obligation.

As noted above, the duty to bargain in good faith requires a party, upon request, to offer reasons for the positions it takes in negotiations. If a company simply does not want to accept a union demand, the union understands what it must do: it must attempt to make management agree by exerting economic pressure through a strike, if it can. If management has other reasons for refusing the demand, such as the need for consistency with other company policies, the union then knows that a strike might not be sufficient to alter management's position and, in turn, it might reassess its own position. Reasons move negotiations forward; stonewalling does not.

Management always knows why it will not accept a union's demand, and so it is not a significant burden to require management to reveal those reasons to the union. If an employer simply does not want to give in to union demands, that is perfectly legal. Then the terms of their arrangement—if any is reached—will be determined by a test of economic strength. If management says it is broke and cannot afford to meet labor's demands, the union is entitled to verify management's "plea of poverty" by reviewing its financial records. (As we will see in Chapter 7, the club owners opened their financial records to the Players Association during the 1985 negotiations.) If the financial records support management's claim, the union will then know that a strike may be futile and could even drive the employer out of business. Conversely, if the records do not support management's position, the union then knows it can use economic weapons to achieve its bargaining goals without threatening the company's existence. Management may not unilaterally impose its own terms of employment until there is a true impasse in bargaining—an issue raised numerous times during baseball's penultimate labor dispute in the mid-1990s, which we explore in Chapter 9.

Collective bargaining is a process designed to encourage employers and unions to reach agreement, even though they are not required to do so. Parties enter into collective bargaining negotiations with certain "preferences." For example, management normally wants to hold down wages, while labor seeks to increase them. Each party receives a certain level of satisfaction—economists term this *utility*—from certain outcomes. These utilities can be represented on "preference curves" or "utility functions." For example, assume an employer wants to pay employees eight dollars an hour but would receive no utility from any wage above twelve dollars an hour. If the union prefers a sixteen-dollar-an-hour rate but would receive no utility from anything less than thirteen dollars an hour, there is no range wherein both parties receive satisfaction from a settlement. There is no overlapping "contract zone," and negotiations will fail.

How, then, do negotiators shift utility functions and create a contract zone? Parties can exchange information that may alter preferences—for example, "This result will be much better for you than you think because it will increase morale and productivity among your employees" or "This outcome will make sure the company prospers, thus assuring long-term jobs for the employees." Another method of negotiating is to package topics together—for example, "if you do *x*, I will do *y* on this other issue." The combined utility functions may produce a contract zone.

A third way to create a contract zone is by forcing a shift in utility functions through the threat or use of economic weapons. The union strike and the employer lockout are as much a part of collective bargaining as the exchange of demands and late-night bargaining sessions. An employer may recognize a utility gain in a fourteen-dollar-an-hour wage rate if it avoids a work stoppage. A union may discover a lower wage is better than losing all wages during a strike or an employer lockout. Through a combination of threats, promises, tactics, reason, and the exchange of information, parties can reach agreement in many instances.

Successful collective bargaining results in a written agreement that binds the parties for a specified term of years. The agréement sets forth the terms and conditions of employment. Generally, the agreement does not guarantee anyone a job, but it normally provides job security through the requirement that management may fire a worker only for "just cause." The agreement sets rules and principles for the workplace, those internal laws that regulate the work relationship. For example, the common measure of preference in promotion or layoff decisions is seniority, but its use is based not on some public law, external to the workplace, but rather on the terms of the collective bargaining agreement.

In addition to legislating these rules, labor and management commonly establish an internal, private mechanism to resolve disputes through an authoritative interpretation and application of the agreement. A grievance procedure, culminating in impartial labor arbitration—a process that had a revolutionary impact on the business of baseball—generally serves as the judicial instrument of the autonomous labor relationship.

Bargaining in Baseball

As a result of the American League umpires' successful action before the National Labor Relations Board, Marvin Miller and the Players Association knew that the Labor Board would protect baseball players in the exercise of their rights under federal law. For the first time in the history of the baseball enterprise, there was a power in the world above the owners and the commissioner; there was the law of the land, not just the internal law of baseball. Federal law, enforced by a federal agency, sanctioned the union's use of the strike to compel management's agreement to improve terms and conditions of employment, required the owners to bargain in good faith over terms and conditions of employment, and protected active unionists against discrimination.

In 1968, even before the Labor Board's decision on the umpires, Miller had convinced the club owners to enter into formal collective bargaining negotiations, the first such negotiations in baseball history. By February, Miller had achieved the Players Association's initial, albeit modest, goals: a formal grievance procedure, with an ultimate appeal to the commissioner; an increase in the minimum annual major-league salary, from $7,000 to $10,000; and a clause providing for a joint labor-management study of the reserve system (a study that would never reach any resolution on this fundamental issue). All these provisions were contained in a written contract, the "Basic Agreement." The agreement also provided that if its terms conflicted with baseball's Major League Rules, the agreement would take precedence.

The first collective bargaining agreement is always the most difficult to achieve, and a signed contract is itself a major victory. Only a minority of union organizing efforts result in a union victory, and about half of initial negotiations result in a written contract. In an industry where magnates had ruled without challenge for nearly a century and where commissioners banned players without recourse, the establishment of the Players Association and the creation of the Basic Agreement fundamentally altered the structure of the baseball business.

In each subsequent set of negotiations, Miller sought to enhance the status of the union and improve the players' terms and conditions of employment. In the 1970 agreement, baseball management formally recognized the Players Association as "the sole and exclusive collective bargaining agent for all Major League Players." In what proved to be the union's most important bargaining gain, the 1970 agreement significantly changed the contract grievance procedure: the owners agreed to have unresolved disputes arbitrated before a neutral, permanent arbitrator, to be selected jointly by both parties. The agreement also raised the minimum salary, decreased the maximum salary cut during an option year and guaranteed a player's right to use an agent in contract negotiations.

Unlike almost all other collective bargaining relationships, negotiations in entertainment industries, which include professional sports, do not directly address the wages of the employees. The collective bargaining agreement sets a minimum salary. The player and his agent bargain over the specific salary within parameters set by the collective bargaining agreement. The players union provides agents with the salary data they need to negotiate individual player contracts. This dual-level negotiation system can lead to conflict; for example, in 1995 basketball players' agents revolted against the established players union. The Major League Baseball Players Association, however, has attempted to work with agents as allies in defending the interests of the players, often steering players to agents who will follow the union's party line.

Although genuine collective bargaining negotiations were a significant improvement for the players, under the reserve system, players' bargaining power for individual salaries remained severely constricted. Limited to one purchaser for his services, a player had only one other option when faced with a salary dispute with his employer: leave organized baseball. There were holdouts, however—most notably the joint action of Sandy Koufax and Don Drysdale in 1966. But Koufax and Drysdale were successful only because without their services, the Dodgers' mighty pitching staff would have been crippled.

Conflict Begins

Miller's honeymoon with the owners had ended by 1972. The clubs balked at the Players Association's demands for pension and medical benefit improvements. The stage was set for the first of what would be a series of economic confrontations in the business of baseball.

Miller understood that success at the bargaining table depended on economic strength. While management might respond to persuasive reasoning, it was much more likely that the hard reality of a "cost of disagreement" would drive the parties to agreement. The traditional method unions use to impose that cost on management is to withhold its members' services. The only strikes baseball had ever experienced were pitches thrown over home plate, but life in the big leagues was about to change.

An employer has the right to replace strikers, and across the American economy, management has used that right frequently in recent years. However, in industries where the work requires specialized skills and there are no readily available, adequate replacements, a strike can keep management from continuing its operations. At times, settlement may be cheaper to management than a strike.

Strikes are not without cost to the participants. Employees on strike do not get paid. While a union strike fund, accumulated in preparation for a work stoppage, may assist employees the short run, a long strike may prove disastrous to strikers and their families. Indeed, a failed strike effort may result in the loss of majority support for the union and, ultimately, in its demise. Further, management is not without its own economic weapons in its battle with labor: national labor policy allows employers to "lock out" employees—a tactic baseball club owners would use repeatedly.

In 1972, the Players Association had to establish credibility at the bargaining table with a demonstration of its economic strength. Club owners did not believe the players would support a work stoppage—an incorrect but long-lived assumption that would prove disastrous to baseball management for decades. Miller followed the wishes expressed by his player representatives and led the players out on strike before the start of the season, the first collective bargaining strike in baseball history. The power of the strike depends on a union's ability to maintain solidarity among its membership. Without a broad consensus across the whole membership of the Players Association, the 1972 work stoppage would have failed, and the Major League Baseball Players Association would have become another historical footnote.

The American public could not (and still cannot) understand how these well-paid young men could strike, let alone form a union. The sports media were strongly and incessantly anti-union in tone and content. Why would these talented and often pampered young men, privileged to be able to play a child's game for an adult living, affiliate with a union and stand by it through a strike? Although we now know that unionization made the ballplayers rich beyond their dreams, this result was not at all clear in the early 1970s when the baseball industry, with a history of ignoring employee concerns, remained bound by a tight reserve system.

Player uncertainty about job security is a primary motivating factor supporting unionization and union solidarity in professional sports. For most American workers, jobs provide a steady, if unspectacular, income. In baseball and other professional sports, management retains virtually unlimited discretion over the careers of the players, and those professional careers, on average, are very short, lasting little more than five years at the major-league level. Management can terminate a player if it determines the athlete no longer is able to perform at the major-league level. Obviously, this unreviewable, unfettered discretion has the potential for abuse.

In addition to their tenuous job security, ballplayers felt they did not receive respect from club management. As Curt Flood wrote in his letter to Commissioner Bowie Kuhn, players felt as if they were "a piece of property to be bought and sold." Baseball players, like most workers, sought an acknowledgment of their worth as individuals. The owners, in turn, did nothing to assuage the players' insecurity.

Through unionizing, baseball players sought fair treatment and a measure of due process. The players believed that owners had ignored their grievances, and they wanted improved benefits. Pensions were of particular importance, because ballplayers in the 1970s knew that many of their predecessors had left the game without the skills needed for postbaseball careers and with few banked resources. Only a handful of stars could cash in on their marquee value or coach in the sport. Most ballplayers lack college degrees and are unskilled, except for their remarkable talent on the diamond.

There was a growing awareness among ballplayers of the possible strength of collective efforts. Without a union between 1947 and 1966, when Miller became executive director of the Players Association, the owners had increased the minimum salary for a major-league baseball player only once, from $5,000 to $6,000. The players saw the association as the means for capturing an increased share of the profits they thought the baseball enterprise generated. After all, the ballplayers provided the entertainment sold to the public.

But why, then, do ballplayers, now enriched by the Players Association's efforts, remain aligned with their bargaining representative? Perhaps they know that all they have achieved can be washed away without the aid of a vigilant representative supported by the membership. Although two decades of unionization have altered the players' economic status, little has changed in the club owners' attitude toward the players. Grateful for prior successes that made their work lives more secure financially, ballplayers have remained loyal to their union.

Such men can still see themselves as trade unionists because they are truly the nouveaux riches. Most come from modest backgrounds. Almost all have served an underpaid apprenticeship in the minor leagues, traveling by bus, not limousine, from town to town. This common experience in the minor leagues generates a feeling of community that blossoms into union solidarity at the major-league level.

Many fans believe the players are greedy, repeatedly interrupting the national game for their personal gain. Many people played baseball as children, a fact that explains the paradox of the public's attraction to the game and its simultaneous mistrust of the players' motives. Fans do not always appreciate the truly unique athletic talents possessed by the handful of men who successfully climb the pyramid of the minor leagues to the major-league level. There are fewer than seven hundred major-league players, winnowed from tens of thousands of minor-league prospects and hundreds of thousands of sandlot hopefuls. Yet Judge Kenesaw Mountain Landis, while hearing the Federal League antitrust suit against the major leagues before he became the game's first commissioner, said in open court, "As a result of thirty years of observation, I am shocked because you call playing baseball 'labor'."

The 1972 confrontation would prove that the Players Association was a real trade union. Some owners saw the dispute as an opportunity to eliminate collective bargaining in baseball and break the union, the first of many such confrontations where management sought to reestablish its dominance in the industry. Eighty-six games were canceled before the strike was settled with the help of federal mediators. The Players Association achieved its bargaining goals, and the formal agreement was signed on February 28, 1973.

Not all players appreciated the importance of the strike, despite its outcome. Pete Rose (a Baseball Law All-Star whose gambling escapades are discussed in Chapter 8) remarked that the 1972 strike cost him a two-hundred-hit season in 1972 because he did not have the full 162-game schedule in which to play. He ended with 198 hits. It should be noted for the record, however, that Rose did play in 154 games that year, the normal quota of games in most years of baseball history.

Salary Arbitration

During the 1972–1973 negotiations, Miller pressed for an end to the reserve system, but baseball management resisted. The owners would not allow the competitive market to determine player salaries. Instead, they offered the players a unique method to resolve salary disputes by arbitration, a process suggested in a 1966 article by labor economist Carl Stevens. Starting after the 1973 season, final-offer arbitration would settle disputes over salaries for eligible players. No longer would players hold out for higher salaries, a common occurrence then (and now) in other professional sports.

Under baseball's unique salary arbitration system, a neutral arbitrator jointly appointed by management and the Players Association selects either the final demand of the eligible player or the final offer of the employing club. The arbitrator may not mediate or compromise. The decision, made within twenty-four hours, is based on criteria listed in the collective bargaining agreement, and the result is final and binding on the parties. In actual practice, the determining criterion is the compensation of other ballplayers who are comparable to the player whose case is in arbitration.

At salary arbitration hearings, held annually either in central Florida or on the West Coast in February, representatives of both the player and the club present the arbitrator with statistics, each seeking to establish that their party's position is the better choice. They offer different lists of players they claim are "comparables" and explain why the arbitrator should adopt their particular comparisons. A greedy player who sets his demand too high or a stingy club that makes an offer far too low is likely to lose in salary arbitration.

Over the past quarter century, management has won more cases than it has lost in salary arbitration. Nevertheless, the system has had an upward drag on player salaries, especially when compared to the truncated market under a tight reserve system, where management could offer a player what it wished on a take-it-or-leave-it basis. Eligible players with the opportunity to use salary arbitration have levered greater salary increases in exchange for not pursuing that process. Given the bias toward increasing players' salaries, in virtually every set of negotiations since 1972, management has sought to alter the eligibility standards for salary arbitration or to rewrite the contract criteria that salary arbitrators must employ.

Salary arbitration has fulfilled many of the expectations of the parties. There are no holdouts in baseball among players eligible for salary arbitration. Salary arbitrators do resolve the disputes, leaving nothing for further negotiation. The parties anticipated the "final-offer" feature of salary arbitration would encourage settlement, and that, too, has worked. The club and the player both attempt to fix their final positions closer to what might be the fair market value of the player's services, determined by examining the salaries of comparable players. This dynamic draws the parties closer in their offer and demand. Each side attempts to predict where the arbitrator will come out in the case and moves its position closer to that point.

Nearly all disputes are settled without need for an actual salary arbitration hearing or ruling. Cases are arbitrated only when the parties have a significant difference in their perceptions of a player's market value, when management cannot settle voluntarily without disturbing its negotiations with other players, or when a player has an inflated view of his own worth.

The salary arbitration system has also had some unintended negative consequences. During the salary arbitration hearing, management's representatives explain to the neutral arbitrator why the player is not worth his higher salary demand. This effort—deprecating a player who is member of their team, one of the club's valuable assets—has a lasting impact on player morale. In addition, experience has shown that a club that loses in arbitration will often trade a player who prevails.

The Impact of Collective Bargaining

Did player unionization and collective bargaining improve baseball? Or did they ruin it? Collective bargaining certainly changed the nature of the baseball business and significantly benefited the players; but did the union's crusade destroy the national pastime? Although the Players Association reallocated the profits of the business, its action impoverished no participants in this enterprise. Owners and players have both profited as the baseball business has thrived.

Nonetheless, there have been negative repercussions. The battle between management and labor had nothing to do with the game on the field, yet it devastated the mythology, predictability, and sense of tradition that made baseball America's premier professional sport. Baseball fans did not care if players were paid a pittance and treated like dirt. They probably would not have cared if players were paid a king's ransom, as long as it did not affect the game.

The incessant management wailing about skyrocketing salaries is as irrelevant to the public as a player's complaint that a multimillion-dollar salary is a personal affront. The fans quickly lost patience with the battle between the players and the owners. As Chapter 9 details, the labor-management conflict of the mid-1990s almost ended the American love affair with the game of baseball.

The private legal process of collective bargaining within the structure set by national labor policy offered the players the means to reap the wealth of the game. Free agency, the paramount success of the Players Association (which we explore in Chapter 6), provided a market for players' services and may even have contributed to greater parity among clubs. The history of the baseball players union does show, in dramatic fashion, how legal processes can combine with the actions of a few individuals to change institutions fundamentally.

Marvin Miller retired in 1983 after seventeen years as executive director of the Players Association. A true power hitter, he changed the business of the game. Although he never fielded a ground ball or stroked a hanging curve, Miller pounded the opposition with genius and tenacity. Through collective bargaining, the threat and use of the strike, and resistance to owner lockouts, Miller created a money machine for the ballplayers that has dramatically improved the lot of his union's membership.

My selfish objective is to win baseball
games. BRANCH RICKEY

5: The Owners and the Commissioner

BRANCH RICKEY

Branch Rickey, a Michigan-trained
lawyer, is remembered for his business
sagacity and humanitarian vision. His
comprehensive farm system and
successful effort to end apartheid in the
national game make him a giant in the
history of the baseball enterprise.
*(Photo courtesy of National Baseball
Hall of Fame Library, Cooperstown,
N.Y.)*

CHARLES O. FINLEY

Described by one sportswriter as
"alternately brilliant, irrational, clever,
devious, creative, and nasty," Charlie
Finley's stinginess produced the first
free agent, and his attempted sale of
the stars of the Oakland As generated a
major court test of the commissioner's
powers. *(Photo courtesy of Corbis-
Bettmann and National Baseball Hall of
Fame Library, Cooperstown, N.Y.)*

Private legal processes control business relationships within organized baseball. For over a century, baseball's lawyers have been as busy as a batboy during a ten-run rally, attending to the business side of the game. Their clients are the club owners who invest in the enterprise. Baseball is a private enterprise, bound by its own internal laws and regulations. It is common for disputes to arise between franchise owners and the office of the commissioner concerning the application of the controlling private rules. On occasion, public, formal institutions, such as courts, will umpire these internecine conflicts, but for the most part, the disputes are handled internally. Because of the importance of baseball's governance structure, our All-Star Baseball Law Team certainly needs a management representative. But how do you choose one magnate from so many colorful personalities?

We need not select a paradigm of virtue—although there were some—but rather a person whose actions played a pivotal role in the development of the business and legal processes of baseball. Albert Spalding's career-long involvement as a player, owner, entrepreneur, and guiding spirit in organized baseball's formative years makes him a worthy candidate. We have already seen how he crushed the player revolt of 1890. Connie Mack, the dapper owner and field manager of the Philadelphia Athletics from 1901 until 1950, deserves careful consideration. He twice built dynasties, only to sell his stars for profit. Or we could pick George "Rube" Foster, the indomitable player-owner who created the Negro National League, where stars flourished despite their exile from the major leagues because of the color of their skin, by a "gentleman's agreement" among the club owners.

Because the choice is so difficult (and there are so many good stories to tell), we will platoon two representatives of management on our squad—

Branch Rickey and Charles O. Finley. The first was a giant, remembered for his business sagacity and humanitarian vision. The second was a showman whose penny pinching produced the first free agent emancipated through arbitration, and whose injudicious greed produced a strong judicial reaffirmation of the internal regulatory powers of the commissioner of baseball.

The Governance Structure of the Baseball Enterprise

Baseball clubs are members of a private, voluntary association—the major leagues—divided into two circuits, the American and National Leagues, each with its own president who retains administrative and disciplinary duties. This is a unique business structure in American professional team sports. Although, as in baseball, both the National Football League and the National Hockey League resulted from the merger of rival leagues, they have integrated their operating structures and play by a common set of rules. In baseball, however, while the American League uses the designated hitter, the National League does not, an anomaly as strange as baseball's exemption from the antitrust laws.

Most professional team sports operate as leagues with centralized regulatory offices, such as the commissioner of baseball. Other professional sports use different arrangements, such as the "tours" in tennis, golf, bowling, and auto racing. Another structure is the annual or periodic "cup tournament," as in soccer (the World Cup), tennis (the Davis Cup), golf (the Ryder Cup), and yachting (the America's Cup). The most prominent of these international sports festivals is the quadrennial Olympics. Each of these business structures presents distinct issues of governance, national and international control, antitrust implications, and unionization.

From the 1903 signing of the National Agreement, which ended the war between the National and American Leagues, until the owners appointed the first commissioner, the National Commission governed baseball. The three-man commission consisted of the two league presidents and a third member, usually a club owner, selected by the presidents. Since 1921 a single commissioner, appointed and paid by the club owners, has regulated the sport.

The Black Sox scandal of the early 1920s, discussed in Chapter 8, convinced the owners that they needed a prominent outsider, a neutral protector of the sport, to maintain public confidence in the game. The magnates turned to Judge Kenesaw Mountain Landis, a pompous, shaggy-haired federal judge from Chicago whom President Theodore Roosevelt had appointed to the bench in 1905. Landis accepted the commissioner's position but continued to serve as a federal judge for over a year, a conflict of interest that foreshadowed Landis's arrogant performance as baseball's high potentate.

When appointed the first baseball commissioner on January 12, 1921, Landis told the owners that he accepted their offer with the clear understanding that the owners had sought "an authority . . . outside of your own business, and that a part of that authority would be a control over whatever and whoever had to do with baseball." In turn, the owners signed a "Pledge to Support the Commissioner," a document unprecedented in any business enterprise:

> We, the undersigned, earnestly desirous of insuring to the public wholesome and high-class baseball, and believing that we ourselves should set for the players an example of the sportsmanship which accepts the umpire's decision without complaint, hereby pledge ourselves loyally to support the Commissioner in his important and difficult task; and we assure him that each of us will acquiesce in his decisions even when we believe them mistaken, and that we will not discredit the sport by public criticism of him or of one another.

Perhaps the owners thought that, as a judge, Landis would feel bound by precedent, custom, and tradition, constrained by a need to decide matters by "reasoned elaboration" from established principles rather than by fiat. For the most part, however, Landis had his own idiosyncratic way as commissioner, exercising instead what might be called a "power of continuing discretion." Because he was appointed to be the savior of the national game, at times Landis appeared bound only by divine control. He was the only commissioner in the history of the game to enjoy such a broad prerogative.

Baseball clubs are privately owned. They are not operated or regulated by government institutions, although considerable public funding supports franchises, provides stadia, and offers other subsidies. As a private, voluntary association, the clubs of the major leagues are bound by a contract that sets forth the rules that govern that association—the Major League Agreement. The participants are bound to the promises they made when they joined the association. As long as the commissioner abides by those rules, the owners are bound to comply with his directives. In fact, as part of the Major League Agreement, club owners and others within the enterprise waive any recourse to the courts to contest a commissioner's order.

The commissioner has broad power to approve contracts; resolve disputes between clubs and between clubs and players; discipline players, clubs, and club owners; and make rules governing the administration of the baseball enterprise. The commissioner's function is to maintain standards of conduct that further the "best interests of the national game of baseball." This guiding standard is interpreted from the owners' perspective, not that of the players or the fans. As a result, it primarily results in enhancing the profits of the club owners, although the commissioner may couch his decisions in terms of furthering the interests of baseball fans.

Courts stood ready to enforce Landis's broad powers, when he exercised them within the elastic boundaries established by the Major League Agreement. In a case upholding Landis's investigation of an owner's stock holdings in minor-league clubs that led to the "covered" player's free agency, federal judge Walter C. Lindley wrote:

> The various agreements and rules, constituting a complete code for, or charter and by-laws of, organized baseball disclose a clear intent upon the part of the parties to endow the commissioner with all the attributes of a benevolent but absolute despot and all the disciplinary powers of the proverbial pater familias.

Major league baseball needed this "despot" to enforce the cartel's rules and to maximize the magnates' satisfaction. Before the advent of a strong players union, the commissioner's word was final and binding on all matters involving the sport, in the absence of extreme abuse, fraud, collusion, or arbitrariness. Courts would not interfere with the commissioner's decisions if they were a legitimate exercise of his power under the Major League Agreement and made in accordance with the procedures set forth in that controlling text. The commissioner protected the "ideals" of baseball. Judge Lindley described Landis's charter:

> The code is expressly designed and intended to foster keen, clean competition in the sport of baseball, to preserve discipline and a high standard of morale, to produce an equality of conditions necessary to the promotion of keen competition and to protect players against clubs, clubs against players and clubs against clubs.

But no one protected baseball against Landis.

Both Branch Rickey and Charlie Finley confronted the office of the commissioner during their years in the national pastime, but with very different results. Through their stories, we can examine the limited constraints imposed by public institutions on privately created, self-policing organizations. It is important to remember, however, that these formal limits do not explain the differing results achieved by our two management representatives in their conflicts with the commissioner. The commissioner has informal powers, the extent of which depends on who holds that office, who is subjected to the commissioner's decisions, and what the economic circumstances demand. Personalities are as important as principles.

The Baseball Farm System

Wesley Branch Rickey's contributions to the development of the business of baseball were monumental. A lawyer trained at the University of Michigan, Rickey was a skilled manager, both on and off the field, whose inventiveness elevated the St. Louis Cardinals' fortunes. Under his management, the Cardinals were perennial champions and a prosperous franchise in one of baseball's smallest markets, which the club shared, during Rickey's tenure, with the downtrodden St. Louis Browns. Later in his career, Rickey boldly revolutionized the baseball business by signing Jackie Robinson to play for the Brooklyn Dodgers, thereby ending more than seventy years of apartheid in professional baseball. Along with John Montgomery Ward, New York Yankees manager Miller Huggins, and Detroit Tigers manager Hughie Jennings, Rickey is one of four lawyers who have been inducted into baseball's Hall of Fame.

An Ohio farm boy with a strict Methodist upbringing, Rickey always refused to play ball or manage on a Sunday, and he banned his players from smoking and cursing. He was a great judge of young talent, even during his tenure as the baseball coach at the University of Michigan while he earned his law degree. As Commissioner Albert Benjamin "Happy" Chandler later said, Rickey knew "how to put a dollar sign on a muscle" better than anyone in baseball. He kept track of his young prospects in his famous little blue book.

When he was the president and field manager of the St. Louis Cardinals, Rickey conceived of the idea of using a comprehensive farm system to develop player talent. Although some major-league clubs had held financial interests in minor-league teams and could "farm out" young minor-league players, none, before Rickey, had developed an organization encompassing all levels of the minor leagues. Rickey designed his system to winnow out, effectively and efficiently, the real players from the mere prospects in minor-league franchises under his control.

Rickey developed a nationwide chain of clubs ranging from the D to the AA classification of the minor leagues. (There was no AAA classification at the time.) He later explained that his stratagem was the product of necessity; the Cardinals simply did not have the financial resources to acquire players any other way. Wealthy clubs in major markets—Jacob Ruppert's New York Yankees, Charles Stoneham's New York Giants, and William Wrigley's Chicago White Sox, for example—continuously outbid St. Louis for the best prospects. The St. Louis club was going broke.

Rickey's plan was to achieve vertical integration: the parent club would run its minor-league franchises to break even, then secure the most talented players on those clubs at practically no cost. The parent club controlled the instruction and discipline of the younger players and therefore could better evaluate their talent and potential.

Starting with Fort Smith, Arkansas; Houston, Texas; and Syracuse, New York, Rickey expanded his farm system to a pyramid of thirty-two clubs with more than six hundred players under contract. More than twenty of the farm teams were at the entry class D level. Rickey also signed "working agreements" with other minor-league clubs and even entire minor leagues, supplying financial support in exchange for the exclusive right to select players for a modest price. He also held tryout camps nationwide and signed hundreds of boys to stock his minor-league clubs.

Rickey's farm system produced fabulous success on the field and in the Cardinals' coffers. From 1926 until 1946, St. Louis took nine pennants and finished second six times. In addition to having the best record in baseball, the financial bottom line for the Cardinals' owners showed equally positive results. For more than two decades, the profits of the St. Louis club were double that of any other National League team, mostly because Rickey's farm system sold its surplus players to other major-league organizations. In one year, sixty-five players who had started their professional careers in Rickey's farm system were playing in the major leagues.

Baseball's authoritarian commissioner Landis adamantly opposed Rickey's farm system plan. This was not Rickey's first run-in with the commissioner. In 1921, Landis had accused Rickey of having "secret agreements" with two Texas League clubs that "covered up" a young ballplayer, Phil Todt. Landis awarded the contested minor-league player to the Cardinals' crosstown rivals, the St. Louis Browns. (Actually, Rickey did not lose much; Todt had an eight-year major-league career as an unspectacular first baseman, hitting only .258 with a career total of fifty-seven home runs.)

Landis had less success when he attacked Rickey's entire farm system. The 1903 National Agreement that had ended the war between the American and National Leagues prohibited clubs from controlling minor-league talent. In 1913, the three-man National Commission, the predecessor to the commissioner's office, also prohibited clubs from owning minor-league franchises, although it never enforced the rule. In contrast, the National Agreement of 1921, which established the commissioner's office, did not prohibit minor-league ownership. As a result, Landis did not have a legal anchor in baseball's governing documents for an all-out attack on Branch Rickey's project.

At first Landis thought Rickey's scheme would collapse under its own weight, because clubs could not afford the expense of operating a farm system of teams. Before Rickey, major-league clubs had left the recruitment of talent up to independently owned minor-league operations, which collected a return on their investment when they sold proven prospects to the majors. Under this system, the major-league clubs had no need to employ scouts or take the risk that a player would not fulfill his potential. Landis (and others) thought that any different system would not be cost effective.

Before the 1920s, nearly all professional baseball franchises were parties to a draft agreement that allowed major-league clubs to select minor leaguers at set prices. When this agreement collapsed, a free market emerged for young players. Major-league clubs bid against one another for proven minor-league talent. Under Rickey's farm system, however, the Cardinals already owned the contracts of hundreds of prospects. Rickey's strategy made obvious sense in this new economic environment.

Although Landis regularly showed open disdain for the club owners who employed him, few, apart from Rickey, dared to oppose him. At the 1927 owners meeting, Landis first raised the issue of major-league club ownership of minor-league farm teams. He said he was very much "agin' it." The next year, calling the farm system the "baseball chain gang," Landis polled the clubs as to their minor-league ownership interests, making his position clear that the farm system was not in the "best interests of baseball."

Landis expressed numerous objections to the farm system. He thought one club's control of so many prospects inhibited the free movement of players up into the major leagues. He also thought the farm system hurt local minor-league owners and the cities and towns where their teams played. Landis announced publicly that the farm system would lead to the "ruination" of the minor leagues, because franchises without a relationship with a major-league club would either have to find a financial angel or fold. Rickey was not deterred, however. He responded publicly that his farm system was "wide open, progressive, efficient and healthy."

The true test of any business innovation is its profitability. There can be no doubt that Rickey's farm system succeeded in the marketplace. Despite Landis's dire prediction regarding the health of baseball's minor-league system, the Cardinals' farm clubs prospered. Eventually, all other major-league clubs adopted Rickey's system for developing talent. Landis was left without a constituency to halt the spread of farm systems.

Rickey proved a worthy opponent to Landis. The Rickey-Landis confrontation showed that the commissioner was not omnipotent. The St. Louis manager was as clever as Landis and as dogged in his approach to controversial issues. In running the Cardinals' business, he focused only on the franchise's net income. Many of Rickey's schemes proved successful. He made opportune business decisions, but as he said, "Luck is the residue of design."

Since Rickey's innovation violated no preexisting rules, Landis used his considerable informal influence in relentlessly attacking the farm system. He watched the major-league farm systems carefully, and when he discovered any illegal movement of players, he intervened to declare players free agents. Landis granted free agency to seventy-four St. Louis minor-league players in 1938 and to ninety-one Detroit players in 1940.

Yet, despite his substantial powers, Landis could not abort Rickey's imaginative undertaking. Undeterred by the commissioner's public pronouncements, Rickey maintained a system that produced an abundance of baseball talent, including Hall of Famers Stan Musial and Jay Hanna "Dizzy" Dean. He sold the contract rights of hundreds of players to rival clubs, earning a substantial profit for Cardinals ownership until he left St. Louis in 1942 for Brooklyn. By the 1950s, major-league clubs owned more than half of the minor-league teams. Today, virtually all minor-league clubs are affiliated with major-league franchises.

The struggle between Landis and Rickey lasted for more than two decades and continued even after the farm system became the common means of developing talent in the baseball industry. They fought the battle within the framework of baseball's internal charter—the Major League Agreement. This document set forth the commissioner's powers, and they were substantial. The commissioner's formal authority allowed him to establish ground rules for the interactions between club owners within the baseball cartel. In addition to formal powers to disapprove contracts and sanction both players and owners, the commissioner, as the appointed managing director of the enterprise, had the informal ability to influence decisions—a power Landis was not loath to use. He saw his dominion as permitting the exercise of "continuing discretion," with no need to treat like cases alike. Some have suggested that Landis often acted simply to reaffirm his power and status as commissioner. Whatever his motives, as the singular guardian of baseball's cartel, Landis was the commanding figure in the national game from his appointment as commissioner in 1921 until his death on November 25, 1944.

As for Rickey, when he was eighty-two a reporter asked him what his greatest thrill in baseball had been. He responded, "Son, it hasn't happened yet." He died in December 1965 at age eighty-three, leaving the game he had loved, nurtured, and altered forever.

The Limits of Public and Private Law

The Rickey-Landis confrontation highlights the boundaries of the legal process. In the ordinary course of human events, persons in society interact without regard to legal rules or institutions. Although there is a tendency to see a legal skeleton in the closet of all interpersonal relations—and we have discussed many areas of private lawmaking outside the formal legal system—there remains a substantial arena of societal life where the law plays no role at all.

At times, human interaction produces harm for which neither the formal nor the informal legal system provides a remedy. The target of a joke may have hurt feelings, but he or she may have no formal or informal remedy for this legitimate, although limited, pain. The victim might appeal to his or her public circle to ostracize the joke teller, but in the absence of unusual circumstances and outrageous conduct, the victim must simply suffer pain without redress.

Recognizing the role of public and private legal processes necessarily involves understanding their limits. Commentators regularly bewail the over-legalization of modern society. Every affront is converted into a lawsuit. Law "reformers" seek to restrict access to the formal legal system, aghast at its misuse by those with frivolous claims. Much of their proposed reform is ideologically based, however. They find frivolous those claims they do not personally value. They often legislate based on anecdotes.

The law reacts variously to the novel claim. Some courts reject suits because they have never seen anything like them before. Other courts acknowledge that the universe of recognized legal rights is dynamic, mirroring the changing understanding in society of the interests worthy of protection. In either case, however, there are limits inherent in the formal law-defining system. To be recognized, new claims must find their analogue in established rights. Although it may appear otherwise to some, the law moves in slow motion, gradually and incrementally accepting new interests for recognition in the formal legal system.

Much of modern life involves the toll of human interaction in a complex society. There is no formal remedy in the established institutions of society for much of the pain. And there is no informal remedy, such as social ostracism, for other affronts to human dignity. Beyond the limits of the public and private law systems, the victim must simply suffer the loss as a misfortune.

In a special-purpose community, such as a business organization, people work according to the strictures of an institutional compact. Written rules and unwritten customs control human interaction. The organization may have a hierarchical power structure that allows for definitive rulings and directives. Even so, personalities, rather than principles, may control.

The Rickey-Landis confrontation demonstrates the limitations of internal self-regulation in one such organization. Landis had no formal power to stop Rickey's farm system plan under the terms of the National Agreement of 1921, though he thought it misguided. Without a private legal right on which to make a stand, Landis was left only with his informal powers of persuasion, forced to act outside his institutional source of power to control behavior. Those participants in the organization, like Rickey, who had the personal fortitude to reject Landis's interference could treat his informal dictates as mere puffing.

If Landis had successfully convinced other club owners not to follow Rickey's lead, the bidding war for minor-league players might have remained intact. But the market overruled the judge. The other owners saw that Rickey's approach made economic sense. They needed to keep him from monopolizing the untested talent pool. They had to follow Rickey's lead or be left behind to suffer the economic consequences.

The Landis-Rickey confrontation shows that personalities and individual idiosyncrasies in human interaction can often be more important than formal legal principles and private contract provisions. In a fight between profit and loyalty to baseball's autocratic overseer, the club owners recognized Rickey's genius and money won out. Most would have buckled under Landis's onslaught, but Branch Rickey did not.

The Desegregation of Baseball

Branch Rickey's most memorable contribution to baseball—and to America—was his successful desegregation of organized baseball. African Americans had played for the early professional clubs in the 1870s and 1880s; among those players were a pair of brothers, Moses and Welday Walker, who played for Toledo in the American Association in 1884. By the 1890s, however, an unwritten gentlemen's agreement among major-league club owners barred African Americans, a tenth of the American population, from participating in the national pastime on major-league franchises. America's system of apartheid that separated the races in all public activities extended to the baseball diamonds. In 1945, Branch Rickey decided to reintegrate major-league baseball; he achieved that goal two years later.

The sixty years of exclusion from the major leagues had not meant that black ballplayers were barred from playing professional baseball, although the organized Negro National League did not exist until the 1920s. Flamboyant black barnstorming teams, such as the Cuban Giants, the Page Fence Giants, and the All-American Black Tourists, sprang up in the nineteenth century. They traveled from town to town to take on all comers, playing (and usually beating) local white semipro teams.

The great Rube Foster organized the Negro National League in 1920, using existing franchises that had barnstormed the country. The Negro Eastern League developed the next year, and after the Great Depression, the Negro National and American Leagues, along with a number of smaller leagues, came to constitute African American organized baseball. The premier event of the Negro Leagues was the annual East-West All-Star Game played in Chicago, starting in 1933. It drew large crowds and showcased the finest African American ballplayers. Because of their financial backing, however, the Negro Leagues were always unstable, and by the 1930s racketeers had infiltrated the enterprise.

Praising Rickey's selection of Jackie Robinson to break the color barrier and his unshakable determination to revolutionize the game is easy, but morality played only a part in Rickey's decision making. Rickey was a shrewd businessman. When he left St. Louis to become the president of the Brooklyn Dodgers in 1942, he saw millions of potential urban African American fans who would be drawn to the ballpark to see their champion athletes compete on the same playing field as white athletes. He also recognized the high quality of the players then toiling in the Negro Leagues, players who could turn around the fortunes of a major-league franchise. As he wrote to a sportswriter friend in 1945, "My selfish objective is to win baseball games."

Although Rickey was inspired by the business potential in the integration of the major leagues, his biography does reveal an early commitment to racial justice. When he coached the Ohio Wesleyan College squad on a trip to South Bend, Indiana, in 1904, to play Notre Dame, the local hotel would not provide a room for Charles Thomas, Rickey's one minority player. "Under no circumstances will I leave or allow Thomas to be put out," Rickey bellowed. Forty years later, he also vowed to do the "thing I felt I had to do" in the major leagues.

The major-league club owners were not equally enlightened, and they were blind to the economic potential of integration of the game. On August 27, 1946, the owners voted fifteen to one (with Rickey's Brooklyn club being the sole dissenting vote) to retain the informal ban. They issued a report claiming that the integration of the game would be harmful to black players and the Negro Leagues. As would become increasingly common during the civil rights movement, white resisters claimed that segregation was better for persons of color.

In this effort, as in virtually everything else, Rickey would have been faced with the unyielding opposition of Landis, a staunch defender of separate and unequal baseball. But fortunately for Rickey's plan, Landis passed away in 1944. It is true that the owners' choice of a former Southern governor, A. B. "Happy" Chandler, to succeed Landis did not seem propitious; but to his credit, Chandler understood that change was necessary for the game. After his appointment as commissioner, Chandler told a black reporter, "If a black boy can make it in Okinawa and Guadalcanal, hell, he can make it in baseball."

After the owners' secret meeting reaffirming the gentlemen's agreement, Rickey flew to Kentucky to meet with the new commissioner. He asked Chandler for his support in the face of the owners' unified opposition. Chandler asked whether Robinson could play at the major-league level, and Rickey assured him he could. Chandler responded, "Then the only reason he's being kept out is because he's black. Let's bring him in and treat him as just another player. I'll keep an eye on him." With that decision, Rickey and Robinson made baseball history. Robinson was Rookie of the Year in 1946, the beginning of a Hall of Fame career. But Chandler would pay for his defiance of the owners; they dismissed him as commissioner after one term in 1951.

Further desegregation of the major leagues was gradual. Although Cleveland's Bill Veeck quickly followed Rickey's lead, signing Larry Doby, who broke into the Indians' lineup on July 5, 1947, as late as 1953 only six teams fielded black players. Boston was the last club to sign a black ballplayer: Elijah "Pumpsie" Green, who took the field in Fenway Park in 1959. And the dismantling of racial barriers came too late for some of the greatest athletes of all time: James Thomas "Cool Papa" Bell, perhaps the fastest man ever to play the game, and Josh Gibson and Buck Leonard, the great power hitters of the Pittsburgh Homestead Grays. Although the legendary Leroy "Satchel"

Paige displayed his excellence on the major-league mound while in his forties and fifties, most white fans did not have the opportunity to see him at the prime of his wizardry.

What made Rickey's dramatic contribution to the game even more remarkable was that club owners had routinely opposed any change in the baseball business. For example, they fought to keep the game daytime entertainment, even after lights became available to illuminate games at night. Evening games were thought to attract a working-class crowd, for some reason an unappealing prospect for baseball entrepreneurs. Owners also resisted the expansion of the major-league game across the country. Until the late 1950s, the sixteen major-league teams extended only from Boston to Milwaukee and from St. Louis to Washington, tiny corners of rapidly growing twentieth-century America.

Race in America

Baseball's "color line" fell because of the courage of Jackie Robinson and the tenacity of Branch Rickey. The complex and often contradictory story of the American social experiment is exemplified by the struggle of its people with the issues of race. Americans are optimistic, even egotistical, by nature, perhaps because we all immigrated to this continent from somewhere else to reap its economic bounty. One group of Americans, of course, came not by choice but in chains aboard slave ships.

The founders of the American republic fought over the issues of slavery, moved more by practical politics than moral vision. The fundamental contradiction of slavery within a free country plagued the nation from its very conception. Thomas Jefferson wrote that "all men are created equal" at the same time that he "owned" two hundred African men and women. In one of many compromises that led to our Constitution, the framers allowed for counting each slave as three-fifths of a person in apportioning seats in the new House of Representatives. Except for their political and commercial value, slaves counted for nothing, not even as fellow human beings.

The nation's greatest war was fought not against some invading foreign army but within the walls of the Republic, which was split asunder by slavery and the economic systems it supported. When the civil conflict was over, but before the ashes could be buried, Congress quickly enacted amendments to the Constitution that formally abolished slavery and gave to all persons the equal protection of the laws and the right to vote. It took another century before these promised rights began to become a reality, largely through the efforts of martyrs such as Dr. Martin Luther King, Jr., and the real threat of civil insurrection. Even then, the prejudices in the American soul that had allowed physical slavery to exist and to continue as economic slavery long after the Civil War remained deeply ingrained. It may take another century to rid ourselves and our nation of the shackles of racism.

The social importance of the integration of baseball, seven years before the Supreme Court, in *Brown v. Board of Education,* declared *de jure* public school segregation unconstitutional, cannot be overestimated. A private, nongovernmental institution that served as our national pastime voluntarily reshaped the social order that had controlled its operation for more than a half century. This visible transformation signaled the coming change in governmental policy and energized the civil rights movement of the 1950s and 1960s. Americans saw their baseball heroes as representing the best in the young men in the nation. If some of those heroes were black, who could then argue that persons of color were inferior?

Free Agency

Branch Rickey's bequests to baseball were monumental; by comparison, Charles Oscar Finley's contributions were meager. But Finley's business escapades are helpful for our purposes, to understand the relationship between the legal process and the development of the baseball enterprise. A former steelworker from Gary, Indiana, who made millions by marketing group insurance to physicians, Finley was described by one sportswriter as "alternately brilliant, irrational, clever, devious, creative, and nasty." He purchased a controlling interest in the Kansas City Athletics in 1960, five years after the club had migrated west from Philadelphia, and moved the franchise further west to Oakland in 1968. He ran the club single-handedly, involving himself at all levels of decision making. He often instructed his manager on player changes during a game, and he designed the As' garish uniforms so that fans could see them from the bleachers. He brought his mule, Charlie O, to all functions and once tried to persuade his ace pitcher, Vida Blue, to change his first name to True. Despite these distractions—or maybe because his team united in opposition to their owner—the As were the most powerful club in baseball, winning the World Series in 1972, 1973, and 1974.

Finley changed the game of baseball in important ways—not necessarily always for the better. He was responsible for the 1973 adoption of the designated hitter rule in the American League, although he did not invent the idea. (It was first raised by the National League owners in 1928 but was opposed by the American League owners.) As a result, for the first time in baseball history the two leagues played the game under different rules. He also convinced baseball executives that weekday World Series games should be played at night, to maximize television exposure. Two of his innovations were not adopted: his easier-to-follow bright orange baseball and a designated runner rule.

Finley taught fellow baseball executives that baseball games were a product that should be sold to the fans. His market sense—perhaps inspired by consummate showman Bill Veeck of the American League's Cleveland, St. Louis, and Chicago franchises—sparked the modern economic explosion of the baseball business. But it was two of his misadventures that warrant his inclusion on our All-Star roster. His stinginess produced the first free agent, and his attempted sale of the stars of the Oakland As generated a major court test of the commissioner's powers.

Finley's As were blessed with truly great pitching. The best hurler was a sparkling right-hander, Hall of Famer James "Catfish" Hunter. (Finley had nicknamed him Catfish because he thought the moniker would have market appeal.) In a fifteen-year career, Hunter won 224 games and lost 166, finishing with a career 3.26 earned run average. He won more than twenty games per season for four consecutive years (1971–1974) for the dominant Oakland squad.

In salary negotiations with Finley over his 1974 and 1975 contracts, Hunter insisted that half of his $100,000 annual salary be paid "to any person, firm or corporation" he designated, in order to defer income and avoid taxation. Hunter designated an investment company to receive the payments, which funded an annuity for the pitcher's benefit after he retired from baseball. Although Finley directly paid Hunter his salary during the 1974 season, he refused to make the deferred payments as Hunter demanded. Apparently, Finley had belatedly discovered that under Hunter's deferred compensation scheme, the club could not deduct the annual $50,000 annuity payment as a business expense in the current year, and that Finley would lose control over the funds. Finley then simply refused to make the payments as he had promised.

Hunter filed a grievance against Finley under the provisions of the collective bargaining agreement, complaining he had not been paid in accordance with his contract. Since 1970, the collective bargaining agreement had provided for the arbitration of unresolved differences between owners and players. While his dispute with Finley was pending, Hunter pitched the As to a World Series victory over the Dodgers in five games, registering a win and a save, after completing an All-Star season of twenty-five wins, 318 innings pitched, a 2.49 earned run average, and twenty-three complete games.

The club owners and the Players Association had selected Peter Seitz as their permanent labor arbitrator. At the arbitration hearing, Finley claimed he had never agreed to Hunter's demand. Seitz found to the contrary. Section 7(a) of Hunter's contract explained the implication of Finley's mistake:"The Player may terminate this contract . . . if the Club shall default in the payments to the Player." Arbitrator Seitz ruled that this provision was "pellucidly clear"—Finley's material breach meant Hunter was justified in terminating his contract. Seitz ruled that because the contract no longer bound him, Catfish Hunter was a free agent. On New Year's Eve 1974, Hunter signed a contract with the New York Yankees for $3.25 million.

Seitz's decision in Hunter's case was solidly based on the uniform player's contract. The obstinate owner had defaulted on a material portion of that contract, and the contract predetermined the remedy—free agency. The case is noteworthy for several reasons. For one thing, it demonstrated for the first time the formidable power of arbitration, the internal judicial system the parties had created. For another, the decision heralded the enormous shift in power within the business of baseball brought about by collective bargaining. The Hunter case also foreshadowed the role arbitrator Peter Seitz would play the following year, when the Major League Baseball Players Association launched a full frontal attack on baseball's venerable reserve system.

The Powers of the Commissioner

Finley also was the protagonist in a major challenge to the powers of the baseball commissioner. After winning three World Series, Finley tried to cash in some of his best players at the height of their market value. He told the *Los Angeles Times*, "We run our club like a pawn shop—we buy, we trade, we sell." On June 14, 1976, Finley negotiated a deal to assign the contracts of outfielder Joe Rudi and future Hall of Fame relief pitcher Rollie Fingers to the Boston Red Sox for $2 million. The next day, he negotiated an agreement to sell ace starting pitcher Vida Blue to the Yankees for $1.5 million.

The Oakland club and all other major-league franchises were signatories to the Major League Agreement. That contract gave the commissioner broad powers. Article 1, Section 2, stated that "the functions of the Commissioner shall be . . . to investigate . . . any act, transaction or practice . . . not in the best interests of the national game of Baseball" and "to determine what preventive, remedial or punitive action is appropriate . . . , and to take such action." Under Major League Rule 12(a), no assignment of a player's contract was valid unless approved by the commissioner of baseball.

After conducting a hearing on June 18, 1976, Bowie Kent Kuhn, the ponderous Wall Street lawyer appointed commissioner in 1969, refused to approve Finley's fire sale because it was "inconsistent with the best interests of baseball, the integrity of the game and the maintenance of public confidence in it." Kuhn stated that he was concerned Finley's greed would ruin the As franchise. A week later, Finley sued the commissioner in federal court in Chicago, claiming that Kuhn's action exceeded his powers and that he had denied Finley due process.

Finley's chances for success appeared quite slim. Prior court decisions had uniformly upheld the commissioner's power to regulate the baseball business. For example, the Chicago federal district court in 1931 had held that the commissioner's power to define conduct as detrimental to baseball was "unlimited in character" and should be "absolutely binding." Based on this precedent, the trial court entered judgment in favor of Kuhn, and Finley appealed.

At the same time that Charlie Finley was appealing the commissioner's rulings, another renegade owner, Ted Turner, the bright, energetic, brash, and self-centered genius who owned the Atlanta Braves franchise, was fighting a punishment Kuhn had imposed on him for tampering with a ballplayer under contract with another club. Turner admitted that he had made remarks at a cocktail party about acquiring Giants star Gary Matthews, at a time when Kuhn had ordered owners not to speak about potential free agents. Kuhn had concluded that Turner's statement was not in the "best interest of baseball" within the meaning of Article 1, Section 3, of the Major League Agreement, and he fined Turner for his comments, suspended him from baseball for one year, and penalized his club with loss of a draft choice. Turner sued, claiming the commissioner had acted beyond his authority; but the trial and appellate courts refused to grant Turner relief, emphasizing the limited extent of judicial review available to a sanctioned party.

Charlie Finley's pending suit against the commissioner commanded a great deal of public attention, but it awaited a fate similar to that of Turner's case. In denying Finley's claims, federal district court judge Frank J. McGarr wrote that the case presented relatively simple legal issues:

> The case is not a Finley-Kuhn popularity contest—though many fans so view it. Neither is it an appellate judicial review of the wisdom of Bowie Kuhn's action. The question before the court is not whether Bowie Kuhn was wise to do what he did, but rather whether he had the authority.

On appeal, the U.S. Court of Appeals for the Seventh Circuit upheld the trial court. The circuit court reviewed the history of the "basic charter" of baseball, the Major League Agreement, and the broad power it gave the commissioner to determine if an act was "not in the best interest of baseball." Under Article 1, Section 4, the commissioner could take any preventive, remedial, or punitive action necessary to protect and defend the game. Kuhn had used those powers to veto the Rudi, Fingers, and Blue contract assignments.

Finley argued that previous commissioners routinely had approved player sales and that Kuhn's action was an "abrupt departure from well-established assignment practice." (In fact, an earlier owner of the As, Connie Mack, had successfully marketed his best players after winning the World Series in 1931, without objection from his friend Commissioner Landis.) In his decision disapproving Finley's contract assignments, Kuhn addressed this claim of unequal treatment:

> While I am of course aware that there have been cash sales of player contracts in the past, there has been no instance in my judgment which had the potential for harm to our game as do these assignments, particularly in the present unsettled circumstances of baseball's reserve system and in the highly competitive circumstances we find in today's sports and entertainment world.

The commissioner was referring to the upheaval in the baseball industry that had begun with the Seitz arbitration award dismantling the reserve system in the Andy Messersmith case (discussed in Chapter 6). Kuhn thought this radical change in baseball's personnel structure warranted a new approach in Finley's case. A wholesale redistribution of talent, the commissioner argued, would disrupt the competitive balance in the league and debilitate the Oakland club.

The commissioner's argument may not have been very convincing on the merits, but the federal court was not about to review a judgment made by the lord of the baseball enterprise. Finley's fellow owners certainly thought the commissioner was correct. Twenty-one of the twenty-five club owners testified as witnesses in the trial court, all in support of their commissioner.

The court of appeals explained that the baseball enterprise was unique in the breadth of power given to the commissioner, and that, in fact, the owners had intended the commissioner, and not the judiciary, "to be its umpire and governor." The circuit court approved the conclusion of the trial court that the commissioner "acted in good faith, after investigation, consultation and deliberation, in a manner which he determined to be in the best interests of baseball," and it added, "Whether he was right or wrong is beyond the competence and the jurisdiction of this court to decide." As long as the commissioner was not motivated by malice, his decision, taken under the authority the club owners had bestowed on his office, would stand.

The Seventh Circuit's 1978 decision in *Finley* is another demonstration of the judicial obeisance to the commissioner that may be unique to the baseball industry, consistent with the judicial tendency to describe the business in mythical terms. Parties to the Major League Agreement are bound by its provisions, giving the commissioner broad-ranging powers. The terms of that agreement are not fully elastic, however. They should be limited by the ways in which commissioners have applied them over the years.

No owner would have possibly thought that he could not market his players' contracts merely because the sale diminished the club's capabilities on the field. Most trades involve economic considerations as well as an exchange of baseball talent. Highly paid, experienced players are traded for young prospects who earn the contract minimum; it would be sophistry to think that current and future salary costs are not implicated by every exchange of contracts. Owners have sold player contracts since the inception of professional baseball.

The only justification for Kuhn's action here (other than that he may not have liked Charlie Finley, which would not have been a valid consideration) was the uncertainty created by the new and unprecedented environment of free agency. The courts were unwilling to intrude into the baseball enterprise to uphold the right that any other independent business has: the right to market its assets.

In the context of the times, Kuhn's nullification of Finley's transactions was understandable and, perhaps, necessary. The business of baseball had been shaken to its roots by the arbitrator's ruling in the reserve system case, and Kuhn's action offered stability to the enterprise during the transition period.

The commissioner of baseball is appointed for a five-year period, and he can be removed any time that he no longer serves the interests of his employers. Landis, of course, entered office with a broad mandate likened to the divine right of kings, but subsequent commissioners have had to worry lest the exercise of their broad powers risked their continued tenure. Happy Chandler's support for Branch Rickey's integration of the game foretold his removal. Other commissioners, such as General William Eckert (1965–1968), were simply incompetent. As I detail in Chapter 9, Francis "Fay" Vincent (1989–1992), the last incumbent of the commissioner's office to date, lost his position because the club owners could not risk anyone inhabiting the perch of power as they prepared for their final showdown with the Players Association.

Bowie Kuhn's sanction against Charlie Finley set an important guidepost for club owners as they entered an uncharted era in the baseball business. The commissioner would enforce the rules of the cartel against those who would profit at the expense of fellow owners. That was why most owners testified against Finley in court: they could not risk a victory for the renegade, even if it meant they themselves could not become profiteers.

In November 1980, two years after the court of appeals decision, Charlie Finley sold the As and retired from baseball. His confrontation with the commissioner had firmly established the primacy of baseball's internal governance system. The owners of baseball teams had established a private club; they could set their own rules, and courts would enforce those rules. They could control entrance into this private club and suspend or ban owners who they thought risked the enterprise. As long as their employee, the commissioner of baseball, followed the procedures set forth in the charter, his judgments would not be disturbed in court.

A Comparison of Rickey and Finley

Why did Rickey succeed in his confrontation with the commissioner's office over the farm system and Finley fail so pitifully over the planned sale of his players? The commissioner's charter was the same in both instances. Perhaps the difference can be explained by the nature of the actions each took in opposition to the commissioner's desires. Rickey's farm system did not directly involve the redistribution of current intraleague player resources, while Finley's sales did. Rickey's restructuring of the player development system was so monumental in scope that Landis would have had to expend much personal capital to stop it in its tracks. By comparison, Finley's transactions were disruptive and universally opposed—except, of course, by the Red Sox and Yankees, who were eager to receive Finley's star players.

Finally, the different outcomes might be explained by the interaction in baseball's private governance system of two central factors that often intertwine: power and economics. Landis was certain Rickey's farm system would collapse under its own weight because it would prove too expensive. Economics would obviate the need to outlaw Rickey's innovation. By the time Landis realized he had misjudged the economics of the farm system, it was too late, because other owners had rushed to copy Rickey's business structure. Finley's player sales, however, disrupted a status quo already shaken by the union's victory in arbitration over free agency. Economics demanded stability rather than an uncontrolled race to the bargain basement. In that situation, the commissioner's interference in the market by using his broad formal powers was welcomed by the club owners.

The internal governance processes of any private business also reflect the personalities of the participants. Kenesaw Mountain Landis would give his friend Connie Mack privileges that Bowie Kuhn would not give Charlie Finley. Landis could not browbeat Branch Rickey into submission, but in that regard he was not alone. Private law and internal governance systems do not apply themselves untouched by human hands or human frailties. The Branch Rickey and Charlie Finley stories show that the baseball business exhibits the same characteristics as all other human endeavors.

This decision strikes no blow emancipating players from claimed serfdom. PETER SEITZ

6: Labor Arbitration and the End of the Reserve System

ANDY MESSERSMITH

A fine right-handed pitcher, Andy Messersmith's most impressive victory came in labor arbitration. His successful grievance led to the dismantling of the century-old reserve system and to modern free agency. *(Photo courtesy of National Baseball Hall of Fame Library, Cooperstown, N.Y.)*

By the mid-1970s, baseball's reserve system had withstood repeated legal challenges. It was clear, after Curt Flood's case, that the courts were not going to address the *Federal Baseball* precedent, as much an icon of a national pastime as "the Babe," even though the antitrust exemption had become an embarrassing anomaly. Congress was equally paralyzed, either by the legislators' idealized notions of baseball or by the onslaught of lobbyists employed to protect the cartel. It would have seemed to most observers that the players' situation was hopeless.

What those observers did not appreciate was that, through collective bargaining, the Players Association had obtained from the club owners another forum, a private tribunal, within which the union could advocate player interests: the labor arbitration process. Arbitration was the greatest invention of the American labor movement, and it proved its value and mettle in the battle over the reserve system.

Messersmith's Grievance

John Alexander "Andy" Messersmith, a fine right-handed hurler for the Los Angeles Dodgers, served as the catalyst for the union's winning challenge to baseball's reserve system. His grievance led to the dismantling of the system, and as a result, Messersmith deserves the starting pitching assignment on our All-Star Baseball Law Team. Although not of Catfish Hunter's caliber, over a twelve-year major-league career Messersmith won 130 games and lost 99, compiling an admirable 2.86 earned run average. He led the National League with a twenty-and-six record, with seven shutouts, for the pennant-winning Dodgers in 1974. Messersmith was never much for statistics, however. As he explained to the *Los Angeles Times* in 1974, "Statistics are overrated. Championships are won in the clubhouse."

One of Messersmith's off-the-field statistics, however, turned out to be his most impressive—an undefeated (1–0) record in contract grievance arbitration. His greatest championship was won not in the clubhouse but in an arbitration hearing room in a New York City skyscraper.

The Dodgers and Messersmith could not agree on the terms of his 1975 player contract after his stellar 1974 season. The Dodgers' owner, Walter O'Malley, renewed the pitcher's 1974 contract with a modest salary increase. Immediately after the close of another superb season in 1975—nineteen wins with a league-leading seven shutouts and nineteen complete games—Messersmith filed a grievance, claiming the owners' reserve system violated the terms of the 1973 collective bargaining agreement between the major leagues and the Players Association. Although the owners continued to claim that their venerable employment system bound players to their clubs in perpetuity, Messersmith maintained that he was free to sign with any franchise.

Once again the fundamental issue of the baseball business was joined, this time before the contract labor arbitrator. Monte Ward's Brotherhood of the 1880s had failed to disturb the reserve system even by forming a rival league; Curt Flood's federal court action to invoke the antitrust laws against the player restraint system proved unsuccessful when the Supreme Court would not overrule a fifty-year-old, antiquated doctrine. With two strikes against them, the players dusted off their cleats and stepped into the arbitration hearing room for one more swing. This brilliant strategy changed the baseball enterprise forever.

The reserve clause—actually a series of provisions in a number of documents—had served as the cornerstone of baseball's labor system for a century. A player could negotiate only with one buyer of his services: the club that retained him on its reserve list. This monopsony depressed the salaries clubs had to pay. An athlete had no choice but to play for the team that reserved him, apart from not playing at all. Other clubs could not compete for or tamper with a reserved player by offering him a more attractive salary. Unless his contract was sold, traded, or terminated, the player remained reserved forever, even after he had formally retired from the game.

Messersmith's grievance claimed that under the option clause of the negotiated uniform player's contract, which stated that "the Club shall have the right . . . to renew this contract for the period of one year on the same terms," a club could renew a player's contract for one year only. Management claimed to the contrary: each renewal of "this contract" also renewed the one-year option clause, which the club could then renew again and again.

The owners and the Players Association had chosen Peter Seitz as their "permanent" labor arbitrator—permanent only in the sense that he decided every unresolved grievance between the parties until either party exercised its right to dismiss him from that position. Seitz was the third impartial umpire under the collective bargaining agreement; in 1970, management and the union had selected Lewis Gill of Philadelphia to serve as their first neutral, and he was followed by Gabriel Alexander of Detroit in 1972. Now it was Seitz's turn.

Seitz was a superb labor arbitrator. He had served a long and distinguished career as a labor neutral before taking the baseball assignment. A lawyer with two degrees from New York University, he had been elected a member of the honorary National Academy of Arbitrators and served a term as its vice president. The seventy-year-old Seitz also fit central casting's image of the labor arbitrator, with flowing gray hair and always dressed for a hearing in a three-piece suit. If our All-Star Baseball Law Team roster had a position for a starting arbitrator, Seitz would be the uncontested choice.

Grievance Arbitration

The grievance arbitration system, administered by a neutral arbitrator, in baseball's collective bargaining agreement followed what had become the universal practice in the unionized workplace. Labor and management know that, during the term of their collective bargaining agreement, disputes will arise over a variety of issues. For example, a company might discharge an employee for misconduct or deny another employee vacation benefits because he or she did not meet eligibility requirements. Sometimes the language in the collective bargaining agreement is vague and uncertain and needs clarifying. At other times, a dispute may arise that was not foreseen at all by the parties when they negotiated the agreement. In all of these cases, labor and management may find that they need the help of an outsider to resolve the dispute. They need a labor arbitrator.

In virtually every collective bargaining agreement, labor and management include an internal, private "legal" structure to resolve disputes peacefully. A grievance and arbitration system allows employees and unions (and sometimes employers) to file complaints claiming a contract violation. Without a grievance and arbitration procedure, a union may feel compelled to strike if a dispute arises over a crucial issue; or it may choose to do nothing until the expiration of the agreement, in which case worker morale and productivity may suffer. To avoid either type of disruption, during the 1930s and 1940s labor and management developed a private method to resolve their disputes without resorting to the courts or using the economic power of a strike or a lockout. This movement toward internal, private dispute resolution accelerated during World War II, when the War Labor Board inserted arbitration clauses into agreements to minimize work stoppages that could have hurt war production efforts. Once labor and management have adopted an arbitration system, they almost never remove it from their contract.

Under a typical contract procedure, an employee first discusses his or her grievance with the supervisor on the shop floor. Usually the two resolve the problem at that stage. If the dispute is not resolved, however, higher-level management and union leadership will consider the matter at advanced steps in the grievance procedure. If the parties cannot resolve the dispute at those stages, the union can bring the matter to arbitration.

The arbitration stage is the first time an outsider is involved in resolving the grievance dispute. The arbitrator is not a judge assigned by a court to keep the labor peace or a mediator appointed to help the parties reach their own settlement. Instead, the parties select their arbitrator to decide the case authoritatively on its merits, in accordance with the terms of the parties' contract.

In their collective bargaining agreement, the parties explain how they will select their arbitrator and sometimes indicate how the arbitration proceeding should be conducted. Typically, labor and management use the services of the private, nonprofit American Arbitration Association (AAA) or the public Federal Mediation and Conciliation Service (FMCS). Both "appointing agencies" maintain rosters of acceptable arbitrators, persons with extensive experience in labor relations who are neutral on labor-management issues. On request, the parties receive a list of seven arbitrators in their region. The parties strike the names of unacceptable candidates in turn, leaving the remaining person as their selected neutral.

Although the AAA and FMCS rosters contain the names of more than three thousand labor arbitrators, only a handful of neutrals is regularly selected to hear cases. These senior, experienced arbitrators, with an average age of about sixty-five, are trained in law or economics. Some experienced companies and unions try to avoid the delay involved in a case-by-case arbitrator selection process and assemble a panel of arbitrators or choose a single permanent arbitrator to hear all the disputes that may arise during the contract term. Typically, they select the most experienced and respected arbitrators, most likely members of the National Academy of Arbitrators.

Most collective bargaining agreements provide for the appointment of a single ad hoc arbitrator, selected to resolve only one dispute. Other agreements require a three-member panel, typically made up of a representative for the union and one for management, with a neutral outside arbitrator. In reality, the neutral member of an arbitration panel decides the case, because the partisan arbitrator favoring the arbitrator's position will join in the opinion, while the losing partisan panel member dissents. Major-league baseball club owners and the Players Association use this form of tripartite panel, with one management representative, one union representative, and the permanent arbitrator (in Messersmith's case, Peter Seitz).

On occasion, the parties explain in their agreement how their arbitrator should proceed to hear and resolve their disputes. For example, they might require that a hearing be held within a specified number of days from the appointment of the neutral arbitrator, who must, in turn, issue a decision within a stipulated period after the hearing. The parties can limit the scope of issues heard in arbitration—a central concern in the Messersmith case, as we will see. Additionally, they can set the rules of their private tribunal or adopt the model rules drafted by the American Arbitration Association.

The parties determine where the hearing will be held—normally at a neutral site, easily accessible from the workplace. The hearing is private and is normally completed well within a single day. Arbitration procedure is informal but orderly. The representatives of the parties—often lawyers, but not always—present evidence to the arbitrator through the oral testimony of witnesses and submit documents, much as in court. The technical rules of evidence, however, designed to keep questionable evidence from a jury, generally do not apply. The arbitrator is assumed to be knowledgeable and experienced, and hence, the arbitrator will discount doubtful evidence, at the same time allowing untutored parties the opportunity to tell their stories at the hearing without much constraint.

After the hearing, parties normally file written briefs with the arbitrator, explaining their positions on contested issues. The arbitrator then issues a written award resolving the dispute, accompanied by an opinion explaining his or her reasoning. The parties' labor contract normally stipulates that the arbitrator's award is "final and binding" on the parties.

Grievance arbitration is used throughout professional sports to resolve a variety of disputes. For example, questions arise in professional basketball and football as to whether a player has reported "fit to play." Under standard player contracts, players injured in training camp or during the season are paid their entire salary, even if they are unable to compete. As a result, the preseason physical examination by the team doctor is a critical step. If a player passes that physical and later is unable to play because of an injury, the injury is presumed to have resulted from team-related activity. If the player fails the physical and thus is not able to compete (and earn his salary), he may file a grievance. Arbitrators resolve these disputes, often relying on the testimony of medical experts.

In recent years, arbitration has grown in importance in amateur athletics, becoming the mechanism preferred to resolve athlete eligibility disputes. Arbitration is used extensively in Olympic sports, for example, in cases involving drug testing. Procedures vary according to the circumstances, but usually they are informal and reach a timely resolution.

Parties use labor arbitration because it is much quicker than court litigation. The time line in the Messersmith case illustrates this claim. It would have taken a court years to resolve this dispute. In contrast, Messersmith filed his grievance on October 7, 1975, and the case was heard on November 21 and 25 and December 1, 1975. Seitz issued the opinion for a majority of the arbitration panel on December 23 of that year.

Parties also adopt arbitration procedures because they are far less expensive than litigation. There is no prehearing discovery, no costly depositions or interrogatories. Arbitration is not cost-free, but parties do save substantially on lawyer fees.

Although arbitration is elective—parties need not include an arbitration system in their agreements—once parties have embodied the mechanism in their contract, courts will force an employer (and a union, for that matter) to use their contract system for resolving disputes. In a series of three decisions in 1960, written by Justice William Douglas, the Supreme Court firmly established the judiciary's limited role regarding arbitration. The "Steelworkers Trilogy" created a "presumption of arbitrability," that is, the courts will send to arbitration any dispute that even "arguably" was intended by management and labor to be resolved in arbitration. Even frivolous grievances go to arbitration, because the parties bargained for arbitration and not judicial resolution of disputes, and arbitration may have a "therapeutic value" for the participants.

Courts also will not disturb completed arbitration decisions if they "draw their essence" from the collective bargaining agreement. When an arbitrator interprets and applies a collective bargaining provision, he is telling the parties what they agreed to. Thus the arbitrator's award is, in effect, the parties' contract. When courts enforce an arbitrator's award, they carry out their traditional role of enforcing contracts, this time in the arbitration context. Courts support private dispute resolution in the labor-management context as a viable—in fact, essential—alternative to traditional court proceedings or industrial strife.

The Messersmith Arbitration

Although fully confident of victory, baseball management did not want to arbitrate Andy Messersmith's grievance; if they could keep the dispute out of arbitration, the case could never be lost. The owners sued in federal court, the venue that had been so supportive of organized baseball through three antitrust actions over a span of fifty years. It soon became obvious, however, that the court would send the dispute to arbitration, as it was required to do under prevailing law. The parties settled the court action, and it was time for arbitration to begin.

The parties presented their case to arbitrator Peter Seitz over three days of hearings in New York City. Players Association general counsel Richard Moss represented grievants Andy Messersmith and Dave McNally. The

Montreal Expos' McNally had joined his fellow pitcher's grievance at a time when the Players Association was concerned that the Dodgers might undercut Messersmith's grievance by settling the contract dispute with their ace pitcher. McNally had retired from baseball during the 1975 season but was still bound by the reserve system if he were ever to return to the game. The Dodgers' boss, Walter O'Malley, the most powerful owner in baseball, was so sure of a victory in arbitration, however, that he stood firm in salary negotiations with Messersmith.

ARBITRABILITY

In his epochal opinion, Seitz interpreted the complex, interwoven, and even contradictory terms of the Major League Rules, the collective bargaining agreement, and the uniform player's contract. First he had to consider the owners' claim that the arbitrator did not have the power even to hear the grievance, the issue of "arbitrability." The parties' collective bargaining agreement contained an arbitration clause that covered disputes about "the terms of the agreement." Disputes not about those terms could not be heard by the parties' arbitrator.

Article 15 of the 1973 collective bargaining agreement stated that "this Agreement does not deal with the reserve system." The owners argued, with some persuasive force, that this clear statement doomed Messersmith's case. If the terms of the agreement did not address the reserve system, and if the arbitrator could hear disputes only about the terms of the agreement, obviously the arbitrator could not hear the Messersmith dispute.

The parties' contract sent out mixed signals, however. The collective bargaining agreement was *filled* with provisions that did "deal with the reserve system," despite the language of Article 15. The Major League Rules, a part of the collective bargaining agreement, included a provision for reserve lists and prohibited tampering with reserved players. The uniform player's contract, also incorporated into the agreement, required the player to abide by the Major League Rules and included the core of the reserve system, the option clause. How could an agreement that created and implemented the reserve system not "deal with the reserve system"?

At the hearing, the Players Association explained the origin of the odd language of Article 15. The Players Association had proposed Article 15 during collective bargaining negotiations while the Curt Flood case was pending. It had been concerned that it might be held jointly liable with management for an antitrust violation, had that litigation turned out differently. (The theory was that if the court found that the collective bargaining agreement sanctioned an antitrust violation, both parties to the agreement might be held responsible.) During negotiations, the union had obtained a side letter from management in which it promised not to change the reserve system. In effect, the negotiations were a cease-fire while the *Flood* battle raged.

In fact, there was little basis for the Players Association's antitrust concerns. If anything, the fact that a player restraint was the product of collective bargaining would insulate the reserve system from antitrust liability. Congress wanted to foster collective bargaining through the National Labor Relations Act. Courts have given effect to this intention by exempting from the antitrust laws restraints negotiated through the collective bargaining process.

Seitz did not address the antitrust issue in his opinion on Messersmith's grievance. He did use the evidence on bargaining history, however, to explain the contractual conundrum—an agreement filled with provisions addressing the reserve system and a provision that stated the agreement did not deal with the reserve system. Seitz ruled that the parties had never intended to keep challenges to the reserve system out of arbitration. Thus he had the power to decide the merits of the case.

THE OPTION CLAUSE

On the merits, the union claimed that Messersmith had completed the extra one-year period of performance called for under the terms of his contract. Seitz agreed, and he ruled that the one-year option clause in the uniform player's contract was just that—an option for one year, and not a perpetual option. He emphasized that his job was to read and interpret the contract, not to decide what would be the best system for baseball. If the parties had wanted to create an endless contract, they could have done so, but they would have had to say that this was their intention. Perpetual renewal would require a "clear and explicit" contract statement and could not be implied from the words the parties used in their agreement.

The harder issue for Seitz was whether a team could "reserve" a player not under contract, that is, a player whose contract has expired. Major League

Rule 4–A(a) established club reserve lists and strongly suggested that a player could be placed on a reserve list only if he was under contract. In contrast, Major League Rule 3(g) prohibited tampering and seemed to afford protection to a club for any player reserved, even if he was not under contract.

To interpret these rules, which pointed in different directions, Seitz looked to the Cincinnati Peace Compact of the National and American Leagues, signed January 10, 1903, which he called "probably the most important step in the evolution and development of the present Reserve System." The compact stated, "A reserve rule shall be recognized, by which each and every club may reserve players *under contract,* and that a uniform contract for the use of each league shall be adopted" (emphasis added). This wording showed, according to Seitz, that the clubs regarded the existence of a contract as necessary for the reservation of players. Of course, since the clubs could renew contracts under their analysis, there would always have been a contract to support the reservation. Nevertheless, Seitz concluded, without a valid contract, clubs could not reserve players.

Seitz opined that the law frowned upon perpetual contracts renewable by one party in perpetuity. He relied on prevailing New York precedent involving real estate transactions, a questionable source of law to interpret a collective bargaining agreement. That case involved a renewal clause in a lease, which the tenant claimed allowed for perpetual renewal, a contorted reading without support in the parties' practice or in common experience. Moreover, the law required greater specificity in the use and conveyance of real property than in other contractual relationships.

In the most important single act in the history of the business and law of baseball, on December 23, 1975, private labor arbitrator Peter Seitz granted Messersmith's grievance and ruled that the players were free of the reserve system. Although later accused by Commissioner Bowie Kuhn as having had "visions of the Emancipation Proclamation dancing in his eyes," Seitz wrote in his opinion:

> It deserves emphasis that this decision strikes no blow emancipating players from claimed serfdom or involuntary servitude as was alleged in the *Flood* case. It does not condemn the Reserve System presently in force on constitutional or moral grounds. It does not counsel or require that the System be changed to suit the predilections or preferences of an arbitrator acting as a Philosopher-King intent

on imposing his own personal brand of industrial justice on the parties. It does no more than seek to interpret and apply provisions that are in the agreements of the parties. To go beyond this would be an act of quasi-judicial arrogance.

Although he disclaimed its moral importance, Seitz certainly appreciated the practical impact of his ruling. He had wanted to avoid harm to the sport of baseball, and he recognized the costs to the clubs of training and season-ing young players if they could easily become free agents. He also knew that improvident bidding for players by owners could result in financial disaster. That is why, as he explained in his opinion, he attempted to encourage the parties to reach a negotiated settlement on the issues. The gulf was too wide, however.

Seitz also knew that the clubs would fire him as the permanent contract ar-bitrator—which they did within five minutes of receiving notice of his award. Later reflecting on his failed attempt to encourage a voluntary settlement, Seitz said, "I begged them to negotiate . . . [but] the owners were too stub-born and stupid. They were like the French barons in the twelfth century. They had accumulated so much power they wouldn't share it with anybody."

ON APPEAL

Vowing not to accept Seitz's ruling without a further fight, the owners brought suit in federal court in Kansas City to vacate the arbitration award. Applying well-established principles of federal arbitration law, however, both the district court and the court of appeals enforced Seitz's arbitration award.

The owners' decision to run to court to vacate the Seitz award was a strate-gic error. The clubs could have allowed Messersmith and McNally to become free agents (as Catfish Hunter had done the previous year) and argued the fundamental issue of the reserve system in some other case before the new impartial umpire who would replace Seitz. Their suit was a futile effort in light of the prevailing precedent. In the "Steelworkers Trilogy," the Supreme Court had drastically restricted a court's discretion when reviewing an arbi-tration decision. The trial court was empowered only to decide whether the award "drew its essence" from the terms of the collective bargaining agree-ment, that is, whether the arbitrator had read and interpreted the provisions of the agreement in making his decision. Baseball management argued that Seitz had erred in reading the contract; but a mere error would not be sufficient to disturb the award on appeal. The court's job was limited to deciding whether the arbitrator had based his decision on an analysis of the contract. If the arbitrator had grounded his opinion in a reading of the contract, the court was required to enforce the award, regardless of whether it would have reached the same result on its own.

Had the clubs not contested the award and had they instead reargued the issue before another arbitrator, that neutral would not have been bound by Seitz's award or his reasoning. Unlike judicial jurisprudence that requires a court to follow controlling precedent, arbitrators are not bound by the rulings of their predecessor adjudicators. It is impossible to know whether another arbitrator would have reached a contrary result, although Seitz's conclusions were far from obvious. Nonetheless, judicial enforcement of the Seitz award effectively foreclosed the option of bringing the issue before another, possibly more sympathetic arbitrator.

There was one other significant result of the owners' suit. A young Kansas City lawyer, Donald Fehr, represented the Players Association in the court action. Marvin Miller was so impressed with Fehr's performance that when Dick Moss resigned as general counsel of the union, Miller brought Fehr to New York to replace Moss. Later, Fehr replaced Miller as executive director of the Players Association, on Miller's retirement from the post.

Analysis of the *Messersmith* Decision

Seitz's decision in *Messersmith* was of enormous historical importance. It marked the beginning of the professional sports revolution in labor relations and provided substantial economic power to the baseball players and their union. It opened the floodgates of free agency, and player salaries skyrocketed in the new free market. The lineage of this financial bonanza stems directly from Peter Seitz's 1975 award.

Seitz's conclusion on arbitrability—whether the case was properly in arbitration—while not without controversy, seems ultimately sound. Certainly, without Article 15, the strange provision that stated that the agreement did not deal with the reserve system, the issue of the arbitrator's power to hear the case would have been elementary. The parties provided for arbitration of disputes concerning the interpretation of their agreement, and the option clause of the uniform player's contract was part of that agreement. Article 15 is troublesome, however, because, on its face, it appears to take the reserve system out of the very documents that have given it substance.

The gates to arbitration are opened or closed by the parties, not by the arbitrator. An agreement by labor and management to use arbitration is not an open-ended invitation to an outsider to "do justice" but rather a grant of limited power to perform certain functions. Under this system, if a subject is not arbitrable, the arbitrator should say so and leave it to the parties to resolve their dispute using other means.

When faced with a claim of arbitrability, the arbitrator must determine the parties' intentions about the scope of their arbitration promise. To Seitz's credit, he did that in *Messersmith*, though it was not an easy question to answer. The Article 15 puzzle could be fully explained by its bargaining history, and Seitz concluded correctly that the case could be heard on the merits in the private arbitration forum.

Seitz could have strengthened his reasoning on arbitrability had he simply stated that Article 15, on its face, did not exclude matters from arbitration. He noted that the parties were skilled negotiators who certainly knew how to exclude matters if they wished. For example, the parties could have specified that issues involving the reserve system were not to be heard in arbitration. Instead, baseball management attempted to use Article 15 to obtain a windfall. The bargaining history showed that the union had proposed the clause to insulate itself from antitrust liability, and it had nothing to do with the scope of arbitration. Management then sought, but failed, to reap a collateral benefit from the provision by using it to exclude from arbitration a dispute concerning the reserve system.

Peter Seitz's decision on the merits of the grievance is much more problematic. As he admitted, not all the provisions of the Major League Rules (which are incorporated by reference into the parties' collective bargaining agreement) supported his conclusion. The language in the uniform player's contract allowed for an option year but did not specify the terms of the contract that governed the relationship between the player and club during that year or whether the renewed contract contained an option clause. The clause states that "the Club shall have the right . . . to renew this contract for the period of one year on the same terms." One might assume that renewal "on the same terms" means renewal on all the terms, including the option clause. Seitz, however, turned to legal precedent outside baseball to reason that if the parties to a contract intended to maintain a system that allowed for perpetual renewal, they should say that. According to the arbitrator, the law "disfavors" perpetual contracts.

Seitz's use of a New York State real estate case is very troubling. Real estate contracts and collective bargaining agreements have little in common. Arbitrators should look to law outside the labor contract only if it is reasonable to assume the parties to the collective bargaining agreement would have known about or considered that law when drafting their compact. Otherwise, external law should have nothing to do with the internal interpretation of the terms of a collective bargaining agreement. Seitz erred: the issue was not what some state court had said in the real estate context but what the owners and Players Association intended in their collective bargaining agreement.

Seitz stated that if the parties had wanted to create a perpetual contract, "one would expect a more explicit expression of intention." Why would this be the case when the uniform contract, since time immemorial, had been considered perpetual? Labor and management add contract terms and definitions to their agreement only if there might be some doubt as to their intention. There really was no room for doubt here, although the Players Association strongly disagreed with the prevailing application of the contract.

The parties to a contract declare their intention in the language of their agreement. The parties could have said that the option was limited to one year only, if that were their intention; they did not do so because they had never reached agreement on this central issue of their relationship. As with many terms not clarified before a contract is signed, the status of the reserve system was purposely left vague because of the pending *Flood* decision.

If contract language is ambiguous—and all language is ambiguous to some extent—parties also show their intention by the manner in which they conduct themselves under that contract. This is called the "past practice" of the parties. This evidence sometimes can tell the arbitrator what the parties meant by the contract's terms. Seitz missed an opportunity in the Messersmith case to look at the consistent practice to interpret the parties' one-year option clause.

The parties' prior practice regarding the reserve system is a compelling indication of their bargain. For the duration of the collective relationship between the owners and the Players Association, and for a century before that, the reserve system had allowed for the perpetual renewal of uniform player's contracts. While that was how the players and the clubs had understood the reserve system, the players and their various unions had contested the system over that entire period. Indeed, in the 1880s Monte Ward had demanded that the reserve system be abolished. The reserve system was not a side issue: it was the core issue that had always divided the owners and players.

Management raised this long history of consistent application in the federal district court in Kansas City when it challenged Seitz's award. Concerning the practice before the advent of the Major League Baseball Players Association, the court said:

> The history of how club owners may have run their business in the 19th century and that portion of the 20th century before they entered into a collective bargaining agreement with a recognized labor organization representing its employees simply is not relevant or material to the determination of the legal questions presented in this case.

The court correctly rejected this evidence for several reasons. First, under prevailing Supreme Court precedent, the court could not retry the arbitration case; it could only review whether the arbitrator's decision "drew its essence" from the agreement. The parties had bargained for Seitz's reading, not the courts', of the terms of their contract, and they received it. Second, evidence of management's unilateral practice before the advent of a collective relationship, while interesting, did not say much about the mutual intent of the parties to the negotiations. What was important—and what Seitz, and not the court, should have considered—was how the parties had conducted themselves under the collective bargaining regime. That evidence was clear and incontestable: management continued to exercise what both parties understood as the clubs' prerogative to renew player contracts. The fact that the Players Association objected to this privilege does not mean it did not exist.

Seitz erred in identifying the intentions and expectations of baseball management and the Players Association as a result of their negotiations. They had bargained over the reserve system issue repeatedly. In their first collective bargaining agreement in 1968, the parties had included a clause creating a joint committee to study the issue and to suggest reforms from the status quo. That committee achieved no resolution, and no one really thought it would. In 1973, management issued a "side agreement," upon the union's request, promising not to change the reserve system. Considering this bargaining history, how could the agreement now be read to have resolved the reserve system issue by limiting a club's ability to reserve a player to only one year? When the parties negotiated the 1973 contract under which Messersmith filed his grievance, nobody at the bargaining table could have stated that the parties had agreed to change the reserve system. Seitz's decision achieved what the union could not accomplish at the bargaining table: it abolished the reserve system.

Seitz also had great difficulty reconciling Major League Rule 3(g) with his ultimate conclusion that a club may not reserve a player not under contract. That rule states, in relevant part, "There shall be no negotiations or dealings respecting employment, either present or prospective between any player . . . and any club other than the club with which he is under contract or acceptance of terms *or* by which he is reserved" (emphasis added). The second use of the word *or* in this provision suggests a difference between being under contract and being reserved. Seitz simply rewrote the provision, deciding the parties meant to say "other than the club with which he is under contract . . . by which he is reserved," omitting the inconvenient "or." Again, this contorted reasoning is necessary only when the arbitrator ignores the parties' consistent practice.

The most important decision in the history of baseball law was wrong. That alone would not have justified the court setting it aside, however. The parties bargained for the arbitrator's judgment in interpreting their contract, and they received it—right or wrong. Management's recourse was to replace the neutral, which they did. Foolishly, management did not bring the issue back to the replacement arbitrator to attempt to obtain a more favorable outcome.

After losing in federal court, management sought to reinstate the reserve system through negotiations; it tried to regain what it had lost in arbitration. But the Players Association stood solid. If the union maintained its economic strength, management could not reinstate its prior player restraint system. Ultimately, the parties reached a compromise: a club could reserve a player for six years before he had the right to declare free agency. Marvin Miller understood that the chaos of total free agency would drive down players' salaries, with players bidding against players. By limiting free agency to those with six years of major-league service, Miller cleverly decreased the supply of available free agents in any one year. As a result, clubs bid against clubs for the available talent. Players' salaries doubled the next year and tripled over the next five years.

Under the new collective bargaining agreement, baseball players have three different levels of salary bargaining rights. Junior players without suffi-cient major-league service to qualify for salary arbitration are bound to the "antebellum" reserve system; they either accept their club's offer, at or above the minimum salary set in the collective bargaining agreement, or leave the game. Players eligible for salary arbitration have considerably more bargain-ing power, and as a result, the salaries of players who reach that level almost double. The third group of players are those who have qualified for free agency. The market of clubs competing for these players' services determines their salaries, and for some, it brings unimaginable riches.

On the third swing, the players had hit a home run—a triumph for pitcher Andy Messersmith, who on the field hit only five round-trippers in 729 times at bat. Messersmith's successful grievance and the implementation of free agency in the 1976 negotiations fueled the dramatic increase in player salaries. When combined with salary arbitration, free agency led to a tenfold increase in player salaries over the next decade. Then, suddenly, the free agent market dried up. It was time for another Baseball Law All-Star to come to bat, and for the Players Association to invoke labor arbitration once again.

Clubs shall not act in concert with

other Clubs. MAJOR LEAGUE

AGREEMENT

7: The Collusion Cases

CARLTON FISK

Carlton Fisk and other free agents filed

a class action grievance claiming the

owners had violated the collective

bargaining agreement through

"collusion." As he had done with so

many base runners, Fisk gunned down

this effort by management to steal back

economic dominance in the baseball

industry. *(Photo courtesy of Corbis-*

Bettmann and National Baseball Hall of

Fame Library, Cooperstown, N.Y.)

In 1985, Major League Baseball Players Association officials noticed that clubs were not making offers to attractive free agents, such as White Sox catcher and perennial All-Star Carlton Fisk. After the spectacular, if perhaps undeserved, victory in *Messersmith,* the union knew that management would have to respond to the new economic environment of baseball. The free market was chaotic and expensive, just as the owners had predicted it would be. The union also knew that whatever strategy the owners pursued, the players could use the labor arbitration system to protect their contract rights. When the free agent market dried up, the union returned to arbitration.

Fisk and other free agents who had not received competing offers from rival clubs filed a class action grievance claiming the owners had violated the collective bargaining agreement through "collusion," by agreeing not to make offers to any free agent as long as that player's prior club had an interest in re-signing him. As he had done with so many base runners, Fisk gunned down this effort by management to steal back economic dominance in the industry. Because of his participation in the union's successful class action grievance, the great Red Sox and White Sox catcher earns a starting position on the All-Star Baseball Law Team.

Carlton "Pudge" Fisk had learned from prior experience that the grievance procedure was effective in protecting player rights. In 1981 he had used the contract system to win his free agency. Under the terms of the collective bargaining agreement, a player became a free agent if his club failed to offer him a new contract by the date specified in the uniform player's contract. The Boston Red Sox, Fisk's home club for a decade, missed the December 20, 1980, deadline date mandated in Paragraph 10(a) of Fisk's contract; it mailed his contract the next business day.

Arbitrator Raymond Goetz found no excuse for the club's delay. The contract was clear and the Red Sox had not met the condition. Hence, although Fisk's free agency was "indeed an unfortunate consequence for the Club in comparison to the minor inconvenience to him flowing from the belated contract tender, that is the inevitable effect of the condition to which the parties agreed" in their collective bargaining agreement—a condition from which the arbitrator "is powerless to deviate." Free agent Fisk signed with the Chicago White Sox, where he would finish his major-league tenure. It was another moment of tragedy for beleaguered Red Sox fans, eternally in pain from the sale of Babe Ruth to the hated Yankees on January 3, 1920, for $125,000 and a $350,000 loan to Boston owner Harry Frazee. (Frazee also pledged Fenway Park as collateral.)

Pudge Fisk was a majestic figure behind the plate at Fenway and White Sox parks during a career that spanned more than two decades. Roger Angell has aptly described Fisk's "imperious" look and "his cutoff, bib-sized chest protector above those elegant Doric legs." Fans will always remember Fisk for his dramatic twelfth-inning home run off the left-field foul pole that won the sixth game of the 1975 World Series, which some consider the greatest game ever played. Fisk ranks first all time in home runs by a catcher and second in number of games played as catcher, and he should be an easy selection for the Hall of Fame when he becomes eligible in 1999. Additionally, the collusion grievance, in which Fisk played a significant role, kept free agency alive for his fellow baseball players—no small accomplishment in itself.

The Collusion Clause

The union's 1985 class action grievance alleged that the owners had violated Article 18 of the collective bargaining agreement, which read: "The utilization or non-utilization of rights under [the free agency provision] is an individual matter to be determined solely by each Player and each Club for his or its own benefit. Players shall not act in concert with other Players and Clubs shall not act in concert with other Clubs." This clause had been added to the contract at management's request during the 1976 collective bargaining negotiations that revived the reserve system after the *Messersmith* decision. Management had demanded anticollusion protection, remembering the joint holdout by pitchers Sandy Koufax and Don Drysdale before the 1966 season. The two superstars of the Dodgers pitching staff boldly told club management that neither would sign a contract unless the club met the demands of both players. Koufax was the game's finest left-hander of the 1950s and 1960s, and Drysdale was among the premier right-handers of his time; both were elected to the Hall of Fame in their first year of eligibility. As a result of their joint holdout, both players received significant pay increases. Baseball management was not going to permit other superstars to ally themselves to achieve leverage at the salary bargaining table.

The union responded with a counterdemand: if players could not collude, then the owners should not be allowed to collude either. Not being able to imagine any situation in which they would want to collude, management agreed to the bilateral promise. The no-collusion provision was meant to ensure that individual players would negotiate with individual clubs. The clause that the baseball club owners proposed would come back to bedevil them a decade later.

During the 1985 negotiation over the new collective bargaining agreement, the owners claimed they were financially incapable of meeting the union's demands; they needed economic relief. Under national labor law, when an employer makes such a "plea of poverty," a union can demand access to management's financial data to verify the claim. The owners opened their books to the Players Association. (In the process, each club owner, for the first time, also reviewed the financial status of the other owners.) The parties settled the 1985 contract after a brief midseason work stoppage. The union agreed to increase the minimum period of eligibility for salary arbitration from two to three years; the owners agreed to readjust the free agency system within a strict time schedule. A team could sign its own free agent until January 8 but then could not renegotiate with the player until May 1. This schedule would keep rival owners from deferring to a player's "home" team. As the evidence in the collusion case would show, however, the owners envisioned a very different system.

The Collusion Case

The Players Association presented the collusion grievance on behalf of all players who had been eligible for free agency. It claimed the clubs had acted "in concert" with respect to the 1985–1986 free agents, violating their promise not to collude. Arbitrator Tom Roberts, the parties' permanent neutral, conducted thirty-two days of hearings that were scheduled over almost a year, an extraordinarily long arbitration proceeding. All told, the parties' evidence and arguments covered 5,674 transcript pages and 288 exhibits.

Both sides knew that the future of free agency was at stake in this case. The market for players, created by free agency, had dramatically enriched the players, but then the goose stopped laying golden eggs. If Roberts were to decide that the club owners had not violated the labor agreement by colluding and that the diminished free agency market was the result of individual club decisions, the players' goose was cooked: baseball management would have developed a legal method to hold down salary increases. However, if Roberts determined that the flat free agent market resulted from collusion among the owners, the players' new stake in the baseball enterprise would be secured—at least for the moment.

Collusion reestablished each owner's monopsony in the player market: if no other purchaser sought a player's services, a club did not need to compete with any other club and could offer a lower salary. Although a player was not required to accept his club's offer—in fact, free agents David Palmer and Juan Beniquez declined their club's offers in the winter of 1985–1986—most players accepted.

The owners' collusion became the functional equivalent of the Lajoie "negative injunction" (discussed in Chapter 2). When Lajoie jumped to the American League, the Phillies were eventually able to obtain a court injunction, but not one that forced him to return to the Phillies. That injunction enforced the promise in the player's contract not to play for any other team. The collusion system did not force the player to play for his own team; it only prevented other major-league clubs from bidding on his services as long as his team was interested in re-signing him. The foreseeable effect was to drive the free agent to sign with his own team.

Roberts focused first on the parties' intention in Article 18(H), the anticollusion provision. Obviously, this clause was "designed to guarantee that individual players negotiate with individual clubs." What would the union have to show to prove the clubs violated the provision? Roberts held that there was no need to prove that the clubs had reached a formal agreement not to compete for free agents. The clause simply stated that clubs "shall not act in concert" with other clubs. Reaching a formal agreement is only one of many ways for two or more parties to "act in concert." Some "common scheme or plan" would be sufficient to prove a violation of the parties' bargain. But what if the clubs were acting in concert because free agency was destroying the fiscal integrity of the enterprise? The reason for the alleged collusion was irrelevant. The clause prohibited any "common scheme" to achieve a "common interest," for whatever reason.

Halfway through the arbitration hearing on the collusion grievance, management fired Roberts, and the Players Association grieved his removal. Another experienced labor neutral, Richard Block, was selected to hear the union's complaint about the arbitrator's removal. Block ruled that under the collective bargaining agreement, the clubs could not remove Roberts while the case was pending. Roberts was reinstated. (Of course, management could—and did—fire Roberts *after* he issued his award, as they had fired arbitrator Peter Seitz after the *Messersmith* decision.)

Proving Collusion

Tom Roberts issued his decision on September 21, 1987, finding the clubs had violated the contract's anticollusion clause by acting in concert. Clubs with potential free agents had acted in a way that showed they *knew* no other club would compete for their players' services. Only when a club stated publicly that it was not interested in re-signing its player did other teams tender offers.

At its core, Roberts's decision was based on circumstantial evidence. Proof by circumstantial evidence is an important element in most cases. Often direct evidence of an act is unavailable—for example, if an eyewitness cannot be found. We can determine the speed of an automobile by the length of the tire skid marks it left on the pavement when the driver tried to stop. We can estimate the age of a person by her appearance. In our daily lives—and in the courtroom—we use indirect proof to establish what has occurred and to draw conclusions by inference.

The Players Association presented at the Fisk hearing dramatic historical data establishing that what had occurred was the result of a common understanding among club owners. In 1984, sixteen of the twenty-six major-league clubs had signed free agents from other clubs; in 1985, however, only one of the twenty-nine free agents received a bona fide offer from another club before his former club announced it did not intend to re-sign him. Prior to the 1986 spring training, as a direct result of the absence of competing offers, only four free agents of the twenty-nine had failed to sign with their prior clubs, compared with twenty-six of forty-six the previous year. As it turned out, the one free agent who had received a bona fide offer from another club while still pursued by his own club was Pudge Fisk, the object of George Steinbrenner's desire. The other clubs had no interest in any of the other free agents.

What caused this dramatic change in free agent market behavior? Was it the product of prudent, sober, rational, and independent business decision making, as the clubs argued? Certainly, many players had been overpaid during a decade of free agency. Or was it the result of a well-understood plan for the owners' common benefit, as the Players Association contended? Could these fiercely independent businessmen really cooperate on anything?

Management claimed the clubs' conduct was the culmination of a ten-year trend of declining interest in free agents and the result of a general economic decline in the industry. Moreover, the 1985 class of free agents was "generally unattractive." The clubs also argued that paying large salaries to free agents made no economic sense (which may, in fact, have been the case).

Roberts dismissed each of the clubs' claims as not supported by the evidence. The historical record showed lively bidding by many clubs for free agents until the 1985–1986 signing season and then virtually no bidding at all. The club owners' denigration of the quality of free agents overall, and of the 1985 free agents in particular, was unconvincing. There were some true stars among the free agents: besides the future Hall of Famer Fisk, the group included Kirk Gibson, who became the National League's Most Valuable Player in 1988 and the hero of the first game of the 1988 World Series. Few will forget the stoic, injured Gibson coming off the bench for the Dodgers' manager, Tommy Lasorda, to deliver a dramatic ninth-inning, two-out, three-run homer to bring victory to "Dodger Blue."

Tom Roberts focused on Gibson's case as a perfect example of an abrupt change in owner behavior that supported the inference of a common scheme. The Kansas City Royals had originally shown interest in Gibson, even inviting him on a hunting trip after the close of the 1985 season. Then suddenly, after an owners meeting in October and a general managers meeting in November, the Royals announced they were no longer interested in Gibson or in any other free agent.

Roberts found that while the alleged unattractiveness of the class of free agents might explain low salary offers, it would not explain the abrupt change in owner behavior and why rival clubs tendered *no* offers. Even unattractive free agents with many years of major-league experience were worth something. More important, the 1985 class appeared to be unattractive only to clubs other than the ones for which they had played during the prior season, and then only until those clubs indicated that they were no longer interested in signing their players.

Roberts was not persuaded that there was a benign explanation for the owners' behavior. He wrote, "Only a common understanding that no club will bid on the services of a free agent until and unless his former club no longer desires to sign the free agent will accomplish such a universal effect." Though Roberts acknowledged that reducing the number of long-term contracts at exorbitant rates of pay for the players might have been a "happy result," nevertheless the owners could not reach this goal by violating their contract with the Players Association. The clubs' economic situation would justify individual self-restraint, but it would not provide an excuse for collusion.

How did the club owners achieve their conspiracy? There was no evidence of a written plan, no "smoking gun." There was, however, evidence of discussions among clubs owners concerning their bidding war for free agents—first in Itasca, Illinois, on September 27, 1985, and later in St. Louis during the World Series, on October 22, 1985. The union presented memoranda and testimony about a discussion among owners, league officials, and baseball commissioner Peter Ueberroth during which the owners were reminded of the evils of "long-term contracts," a euphemism for competitive bidding on free agents. The director of the owners' player relations committee, Lee MacPhail, implored owners to "exercise more self-discipline in making their operating decisions" and to resist pressure and temptation to "give in to the unreasonable demands of experienced marginal players." MacPhail continued:

> We must stop daydreaming that one free agent signing will bring a pennant. Somehow we must get our operations back to the point where a normal year for the average team at least results in a break-even situation, so that Clubs are not

led to make rash moves in the vain hope that they might bring a pennant and a resulting change in their financial position. This requires resistance to fan and media pressure and is not easy.

No one objected when Commissioner Ueberroth told the owners to give MacPhail's comments "serious consideration," to keep "it" under control. After an informal poll was taken, "certain club representatives stated their intent to avoid long-term contracts."

At a meeting in Tarpon Springs, Florida, on November 6, 1985, Ueberroth told the general managers of the clubs that it was "not smart to sign long term contracts." Finally, on December 11, 1985, at the annual major-league baseball meeting in San Diego, MacPhail distributed a list of free agents and offered similar advice. Apparently, the owners listened.

The pattern of the clubs' subsequent behavior was compelling evidence, and the data about the delayed timing of offers was convincing. There was no other reasonable explanation for the owners' parallel behavior. Roberts concluded the owners had colluded in violation of the collective bargaining agreement.

When asked how these independent, opinionated, often petulant business owners could work together on anything, retired union executive director Marvin Miller reminded a reporter that their predecessors had effectively maintained an all-white enterprise for decades until 1947, based on an unwritten gentlemen's agreement, despite the availability of extraordinary talent in the Negro Leagues and an untapped market of fans eager to watch the best-quality baseball. That, too, Miller said, was an informal "collusive conspiracy."

In a subsequent order issued on January 22, 1988, Roberts ruled that the seven named grievants, including All-Star Fisk, were now free agents. He later issued a "preliminary award," requiring management to pay the affected free agents $10.5 million in back pay—the difference between the amount the players would have earned in a competitive free agency marketplace without collusion and what they actually earned.

Roberts's opinion in the collusion case was solidly grounded in the evidence. He skillfully addressed each of management's defenses, some of which were preposterous on their face. Unlike *Messersmith*, there was no question about what the parties' contract meant. The only real issue was what the club owners had done, and Roberts's factual conclusions on that matter were certainly reasonable. There was no other satisfactory explanation for the owners' dramatic change in behavior.

Although fired by the owners as their permanent arbitrator, Roberts continued his involvement in the collusion case. The Players Association appointed Roberts to decide how the millions of dollars of damages awarded in his and subsequent collusion cases should be divided among the players. That process has taken years and is not yet completed.

Collusion II and III

The union also filed grievances alleging collusion among club owners regarding the 1986 and 1987 classes of free agents. In a sternly worded eighty-one-page opinion in "Collusion II," issued on August 31, 1988, arbitrator George Nicolau found a "patent pattern" of bid rigging by the clubs that "defied fair play" and the free market. For the 1986–1987 season of free agents, "there was no vestige of a free market."

Nicolau found that American League president Bobby Brown and two American League club owners had pressured Phillies owner Bill Giles not to sign free agent Lance Parrish, one of the two players who subsequently switched teams by taking pay cuts. Giles eventually signed Parrish to a contract that reduced his pay by $50,000 and included a provision expressly releasing the Phillies from liability for any collusion. The other free agent to move, Andre Dawson, signed a blank contract that resulted in a $547,000 pay cut. According to Nicolau, the owners made offers to free agents "for public relations purposes" only. Once again, except for Parrish and Dawson, free agents switched teams only after their former clubs indicated they no longer sought their services.

Nicolau wrote that the "evidence convincingly establishes everyone knew there was supposed to be no bidding before January 8 for free agents coveted by their former teams." In an unusually candid comment, Nicolau noted that owners suffered "remarkable lapses of memory" in their testimony at the arbitration hearing. Ueberroth rejected Nicolau's ultimate conclusion, claiming that the "owners couldn't collude on where to eat breakfast." When he left the commissioner's office on April 1, 1989, Ueberroth said that he hoped the clubs would not return to self-destructive financial habits and voiced concern about increases in players' salaries. Asked by reporters if his warnings to owners to spend more wisely had led to their collusive behavior, Ueberroth said, "Sure."

On July 16, 1990, Nicolau issued the third and final opinion on the union's collusion claims. He found that an "Information Bank" created by baseball management allowed owners to rig bids to free agents and keep offers reasonable. "The Bank's message was plain—if we must go into that market and bid, then let's quietly cooperate by telling each other what the bids are. If we do that, prices won't get out of line and no club will be hurt too much." According to the arbitrator, this cooperation, which created a "safe bidding environment," violated the anticollusion provision.

On September 17, 1990, arbitrator Nicolau ordered the club owners to pay affected players $102.5 million in damages for the 1987 and 1988 contract violations, the largest damage award in sports history. On December 5, 1990, the owners and the Players Association settled all outstanding claims, and the clubs agreed to make a single $280 million payment to compensate players for contract violations.

Nicolau's opinions stretched the contract's anticollusion promise. The parties intended the clause to prohibit collusive conduct, but should that cover the mere exchange of information? In fact, in the first collusion case Roberts wrote that the owners "remain free to exchange information" at their meetings. Evidence at the Collusion III hearing, however, focused on what owners did with the information they exchanged. Owners kept meticulous records of "withdrawals" of information from the Information Bank. Based on that data, the union was able to establish a direct link between that bank and the free agent bidding process. Owners used that information to "fix prices," that is, to establish their offers to free agents. For example, if one club knew a rival club was offering only a two-year contract at a certain salary level to a particular free agent, then it need not accede to the player's agent's demand for a three-year agreement at a higher salary. Management claimed at the hearing that the players, through their agents and the union, had regularly shared information about competing offers, but it could not prove its claim.

The critical guidepost for an impartial arbitrator should always be the intention of the parties. What did the club owners and players want to achieve by banning collusion? Obviously, management wanted to stop a repeat of the Koufax-Drysdale joint holdout. The union sought to stop concerted action by the owners that would undermine a free market. Through creative use of ex-changed information, management found another way to facilitate collusion, and baseball's arbitrator found another basis for a contract violation.

Arbitration "Technicalities"

Although labor arbitration was designed to avoid legal complexities, some pre-cepts from the judicial system have crept into the private system of adjudica-tion. For example, the arbitrator generally swears in the witnesses, although there are no reported instances of anyone being charged with perjury based on a false statement made in a private arbitration proceeding. Representatives of the parties make opening statements to the arbitrator and then examine wit-nesses much as in a court proceeding, with direct examination followed by cross-examination. The complex rules of evidence, however, do not apply.

For reasons lost in the antiquity of modern labor arbitration, management proceeds first in presenting its evidence in a case involving the discharge or discipline of an employee. This does seem to make sense, because manage-ment knows why it took the disciplinary action. Making management explain its decision seems fair. In all other cases alleging contract violations (for ex-ample, a case involving holiday pay or seniority), the union goes first. In these cases, the union claims management erred in some way. Again, it makes sense to require the union, which brought the dispute to arbitration, to show the basis for its claim.

After the completion of the arbitration hearing, the parties normally file briefs with the arbitrator, although no rule requires them to do so. Those briefs state the relevant facts and controlling principles according to the par-tisan perspective of each side. The arbitrator then issues an award resolving the dispute and a written opinion explaining the reasons for the decision.

Arbitrators, employers, and unions often become entangled in the legalis-tic thicket of trying to determine the "quantum of proof" required to estab-lish a contract violation. Some arbitrators say that management must prove "just cause" for its decision to discharge an employee "beyond a reasonable doubt," adopting the standard used in the criminal courts. Those arbitrators boldly proclaim that a discharge is "industrial capital punishment." While the metaphor is stylistically captivating, it has no basis in fact. Losing a job is a serious matter, but it does not end an employee's life. Other arbitrators prefer a lesser standard of "clear and convincing evidence." This, too, is a criterion that has no intrinsic meaning. What is "clear"? How much evidence does it require to be "convinced"? Union grievances claiming contract violations, in contrast, are almost universally judged by a simple "preponderance of the evidence" standard.

It seems that labor arbitrators sometimes employ these verbal formulations to rationalize their awards upholding or denying a grievance. A discharge that seems too harsh can be more easily set aside in arbitration if the arbitrator first announces in his opinion that management was required to prove its allegations against the employee "beyond a reasonable doubt." Alas, management failed to do so. The arbitrator can hide behind the burden and quantum of proof rather than face the issue forthrightly and rule that management's action was not for "just cause," plain and simple.

The growth of unionization and binding arbitration in the public sector raises the risk that additional legal technicalities will transform the private, informal nature of labor arbitration. In many cases involving government employers and unions representing government workers, the parties ask their arbitrator to interpret and apply state or federal statutes and administrative regulations. Lawyers may fight to import judicial technicalities into the arbitration process when they think it would help their client's case. Over the coming decades, labor arbitration will face the challenge of maintaining its original conception as an informal dispute resolution method and avoiding creeping legalisms that would transform the process into just a courtlike alternative to litigation in state or federal tribunals.

The End of Collusion

Fisk's class action collusion grievance ended another important phase in the history of the business of baseball. The owners attempted to stop the dramatic increase in player salaries through private cooperation. Their efforts, however, clashed with the contract promise they had made to the players not to collude. It is ironic that the owners ran afoul of the salary-setting limitation they had proposed. The collective bargaining agreement marked out the forbidden zone, but owners had other, permissible strategies. Had they acted individually and not in combination, they could have attempted to hold down the increase in player salaries. The dynamics of the free market, however, and the lure of a pennant riding on the shoulders of just one more free agent superstar made individual strategies unmanageable and ineffective.

The owners' common strategy violated a provision of the collective agreement. It was not "illegal" in the same way it would have been if they had robbed a convenience store. The collusion did not subject them to criminal liability or imprisonment. Nor was it "immoral." The owners were not sinners, only contract violators.

The owners had been acting only naturally in cooperating, following a tradition in baseball that started in the 1880s when the Brush Classification Plan imposed a truncated wage scale for all National League players, and even before that when National League clubs first "reserved" their players. The whole structure of the organized game depended on cooperation among the entrepreneurs. However, now the players had a union, a collective bargaining agreement, and an internal "judicial" system to police the promises made by the owners. This framework provided an effective counterbalance to the power of the modern-day magnates.

When collusion ended, player salaries leaped once again, from an average annual salary of $430,000 in 1988 to more than $1 million by 1992. The owners, however, were the beneficiaries of a new television contract, negotiated by Peter Ueberroth before he left the commissioner's office—a deal with CBS that produced $1.6 billion.

The union successfully sought power within the business of baseball at the bargaining table, backed by its surprising demonstration of economic strength. Success then exploded with an arbitration victory that dismantled the reserve system. The collusion arbitration cases proved the clubs could not act cooperatively to reestablish their monopsony over player salaries. The owners knew their only recourse was through the use of their economic power within the negotiation process.

The club owners vowed to change the terms of the basic agreement with the union. If they were to reap the full rewards for their investment in the baseball business, they needed to rewrite the charter of the enterprise. The union knew it had to be equally steadfast if it was to protect the extraordinary gains it had achieved for its membership. The result was the baseball labor strife of the 1990s that almost crushed the national pastime (chronicled in Chapter 9).

Return to Negotiations

Baseball owners had watched while National Football League management effectively dismantled their Players Association during their 1987 labor dispute. Holding fast in their negotiating position and hiring replacement players, the owners had crippled their union, as that sport's superstars crossed the picket line. Thus, as the 1990 baseball negotiations began, baseball management stated publicly it was ready to restructure its entire salary system.

Management had amassed a $200 million war chest and a $130 million line of credit to fight the coming labor war. On February 15, 1990, the owners closed spring training camps and locked out the ballplayers. For management, it was time to play economic hardball at the bargaining table.

Management's bargaining proposals were revolutionary, calling for a wage scale based on performance for players with less than six years experience, thereby eliminating salary arbitration and the need for individual player agents. Owners and players would share available revenue under a salary cap similar to that adopted by the National Basketball Association and its players union, to halt the rise of player salaries.

But then, one week after the camps closed, the owners dropped their dramatic restructuring proposals. Baseball commissioner Fay Vincent entered the bargaining. The 1990 negotiations ended with a whimper, without significant change in the system. The final issue dividing the parties was player eligibility for salary arbitration. They compromised on their differences, and the 1990 season began a few days late.

Interestingly, the 1990 collective bargaining agreement contained increased protection for the players against owner collusion. The contract allowed the permanent arbitrator to award treble damages to a grievant injured through collusion. The contract remedy now mirrored the remedy available to players in all other sports under the federal antitrust laws. Almost seventy years after Justice Oliver Wendell Holmes carved out an exemption from those laws for professional baseball, Executive Director Don Fehr and the Major League Baseball Players Association had duplicated antitrust's protection and remedies under baseball's collective bargaining agreement.

> Baseball . . . must ascend and aspire to
> the highest principles—of integrity,
> of professionalism, of performance, of
> fair play within its rules.
>
> COMMISSIONER BART GIAMATTI

8: The Crimes of Baseball

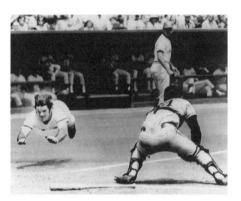

PETE ROSE

Always playing with abandon, baseball's all-time hit leader gambled once too often. Riding an express train to Cooperstown's Hall of Fame, Pete Rose was derailed by allegations that he had bet on baseball games in which he managed. *(Photo courtesy of Corbis-Bettmann and National Baseball Hall of Fame Library, Cooperstown, N.Y.)*

Throughout its history, the national pastime has had its dark side. Periodically, the field of dreams has taken on the characteristics of a nightmare. Gambling plagued organized baseball from its earliest days. Players have abused alcohol and, more recently, illegal drugs. Because it seeks out the public's attention, the game has suffered from public disclosure of the human failures of some of its participants.

Wagering and substance abuse are not unique to baseball, of course. From ancient times, gamblers have sought out human activity on which odds could be placed. Baseball is a very public enterprise, where gamblers can easily ascertain results in the morning newspaper. In addition, throughout much of the history of the sport, owners underpaid ballplayers; as a result, participants in the sport were susceptible to bribes to affect the outcome of the games in which they played. With the advent of large player salaries, the rich young men of baseball could afford recreational drugs and no longer needed to settle for the local brew, a staple of a ballplayer's diet since the early days of the professional game. We acknowledge the bilious underbelly of the business of baseball by the selection of our next Baseball Law All-Star, the indomitable Peter Edward Rose.

Pete Rose of Cincinnati's "Big Red Machine" was the modern game's greatest hitter. In twenty-four years with the Reds, and later in his career with the Phillies and the Expos, "Charlie Hustle" amassed 4,256 base hits, surpassing the mark held for decades by Ty Cobb. Rose also set the record for most games played—a prodigious 3,562—and most at bats, with 14,053. He managed his hometown Reds from 1984 until 1989. Riding an express train to Cooperstown's Hall of Fame, Rose was derailed by allegations that he gambled on baseball games.

A History of Gambling and Baseball

To understand the Rose saga and the actions of three commissioners of baseball toward him, we must review the history of the sordid side of the national pastime. Baseball before the turn of the century was filled with stories of the connection between players and gamblers. Game-fixing, called "hippodroming," was common by the 1870s. Gambling on games was ubiquitous. Brooklyn and Philadelphia even allowed open betting pools in their parks, as racetracks and jai alai frontons do today.

In 1878, William Hulbert's National League banned four players for life for throwing games, termed "conduct in contravention of the object of the league." The prior year the Louisville Grays had led the league until the team made its last eastern trip. The club then lost seven straight games. An investigation revealed that the "Louisville Four" had been paid $100 each to lose the pennant. Baseball executives knew that any association with the underworld could destroy baseball's guise of Victorian propriety, the public image the business sought to maintain. Any players who imperiled that pretense would be banned for life, and the four stars of the Louisville nine were the first to suffer that penalty.

The nadir of baseball's connection with gambling was the infamous "Black Sox" scandal, a story that tells us much about the state of owner-player relations in the sport and the powerful role of the commissioner's office created in its wake. White Sox owner Charles Comiskey paid his players the lowest salaries in the league; they were ripe for the picking by professional gamblers. While the facts remain controverted, it appears that eight White Sox players met with various gamblers, who offered them bribes to throw the 1919 World Series. At least some of these players deliberately tried to lose the first two and the eighth games of the best-of-nine series with the Cincinnati Reds. Seven of the eight players received payoffs. On October 22, 1920, a year after the White Sox lost the World Series, a Chicago grand jury indicted eight players and accused them of accepting payments from notorious gambler Arnold Rothstein to throw the series. (Curiously, four days later the same grand jury exonerated Rothstein after he appeared before them to state that he loved baseball, "our national game.")

Although White Sox owner Comiskey had quashed allegations of a fixed World Series for a while, two players, pitcher Eddie Cicotte and the great slugger "Shoeless Joe" Jackson, later confessed. The nation followed the circus criminal trial through the summer of 1921. The transcripts of the players' confessions, however, somehow disappeared. On August 2, 1921, a Chicago jury acquitted the eight so-called Black Sox, and no one went to jail.

The magnates of the game appreciated the serious threat the Black Sox scandal posed to the business of baseball. Fans attended games to enjoy the superior athletic performance of extraordinarily talented young men. At its core, this meant the outcome of games had to be based "on the merits of play," unaffected by any external forces—such as bribes. The game had to remain free of taint if it was to attract spectators. Gambling risked the economic viability of the baseball cartel.

Faced with a crisis of public confidence, the owners acted forcefully to protect the legitimacy and profitability of their business enterprise. The National Agreement of 1903 had established a three-member National Commission, made up of the presidents of each league and a mutually acceptable third member. It proved incapable of protecting the purity of the sport, however. The owners acted quickly to create an office of the commissioner, a strong, ostensibly neutral governor of the game who could act "in the best interests of baseball" to prevent abuses that had been a regular part of the business since its inception. They needed a trusted person to promote and protect their interest in the sportsmanlike conduct of the national game.

As we have seen, after considering several candidates, including former president William Howard Taft and General John J. Pershing, the owners selected federal judge Kenesaw Mountain Landis, a hero of the owners' winning battle against the rival Federal League, to fill the commissioner's chair. It was a fateful choice for many reasons. Landis would dominate the game until his death in 1944.

Landis believed that baseball was central to the American ethos and that his role was to act as surety for future generations of American youth:

> Baseball is something more than a game to an American boy; it is his training field for life work. Destroy his faith in its squareness and honesty and you have destroyed something more; you have planted suspicion of all things in his heart.

It was not surprising, then, that Landis acted decisively to address the Black Sox scandal as his first notable act in a two-decade reign over the national game. The *Sporting News* reported on January 21, 1921:

> Judge Landis in accepting office outlined his plans for the government of the game, dwelling particularly on the big reason for him entering into it, which is to clean out the crookedness and the gambling responsible for it and keep the sport above reproach. The Judge made it plain he would have no mercy on any man in baseball, be he magnate or player, whose conduct was not strictly honest. They must avoid even the appearance of evil or feel the iron hand of his power to throw them out of any part of the game. The Judge will be the absolute ruler of the game.

Landis's first act was to move the Black Sox story off the sports pages by punishing the players involved. The day after their acquittal, Landis banned the eight ballplayers from organized baseball for life:

> Regardless of the verdict of juries, no player that throws a ball game, no player that entertains proposals or promises to throw a game, no player that sits in a conference with a bunch of crooked players and gamblers where the ways and means of throwing games are discussed, and does not promptly tell his club about it, will ever again play professional baseball.

Included in the banned group of players was one singular competitor, outfielder "Shoeless Joe" Jackson, who, over his thirteen-year career, hit .356, the third highest career average ever, behind only Ty Cobb and Rogers Hornsby. When Cleveland fans once heckled the uneducated Jackson by asking him if he could spell *illiterate,* Jackson powered a pitch to the outfield wall and responded from third base, "Hey, big mouth, how do you spell triple?" After the scandal, it is said that a young lad approached the legendary Jackson on the steps of the courthouse at the Black Sox trial and pleaded, "Say it ain't so, Joe." Unfortunately, Jackson had to say that it was so.

During his tenure, Landis vigilantly enforced baseball's rules against gambling and fixing games. Using his absolute power, he steadfastly enforced the cartel's control. He was not always as strict with all the owners, however; they paid his substantial salary, after all. Landis's autocratic administration managed to relieve the public's anxiety about the legitimacy of the sport, and with the timely assistance of Babe Ruth's mighty bat, the game flourished as never before.

Rose versus the Commissioner of Baseball

In light of the above, we can understand the reaction of three commissioners of baseball to allegations that Pete Rose had gambled on some of the baseball games he managed. The commissioner's office had a sixty-year-old rule that called for life banishment from the game for anyone involved in such misconduct. After receiving allegations in late February 1989 that Rose had violated this fundamental tenet of the game, Commissioner Peter Ueberroth publicly announced that he was investigating Pete Rose.

Rose flatly denied the accusations with an unfortunate choice of words: "I'd be willing to bet you, if I was a betting man, that I have not bet on baseball." The outrage against the commissioner's decision to investigate was particularly evident in Cincinnati, where Rose was so celebrated that the city council once had tried to declare him a "civic monument" to prevent him from playing for another club. It later renamed the road to Riverfront Stadium in his honor.

The commissioner was given the power to investigate allegations, such as those involving gambling, under Article 1, Section 2 of the Major League Agreement. Major League Rule 21(d) provided:

BETTING ON BALL GAMES. Any player, umpire or club or league official or employee who shall bet any sum whatsoever upon any baseball game in connection with which the bettor has no duty to perform, shall be declared ineligible for one year. Any player, umpire or club or league official or employee who shall bet any sum whatsoever upon any baseball game in connection with which the bettor has a duty to perform shall be declared permanently ineligible.

On March 6, 1989, Peter Ueberroth appointed New York attorney John W. Dowd as special counsel to conduct the Rose investigation. Two months later, Dowd submitted a 225-page report to the commissioner detailing Rose's betting. Dowd concluded:

In order to protect his stature as one of the most famous baseball players in major league history, Pete Rose employed middlemen to place bets for him with bookmakers and at the racetrack and to pay gambling losses and collect gambling winnings, thus concealing his gambling activities.

Dowd submitted seven volumes of evidence to the commissioner to accompany his report, including betting sheets that handwriting experts determined

Rose had signed and records of telephone calls Rose had made to known book-
ies immediately before baseball games. While Rose had bet on his own ball
club, Dowd concluded that at least he had always bet on the Reds to win.

Ueberroth's successor as commissioner, A. Bartlett Giamatti, former president of Yale University and a scholar of classical literature, continued the
Rose investigation. On April 18, 1989, Giamatti made an error of Odyssean
proportions. He sent a letter to Judge Carl Rubin, who was about to sentence
Ron Peters, one of Rose's alleged gambling connections and bagmen. Giamatti suggested leniency for Peters, since he had been "candid, forthright and
truthful" with baseball's investigators, providing "critical sworn testimony
about Mr. Rose and his associates." Rubin, a Cincinnati federal judge and
longtime Reds fan, was incensed by what he termed the commissioner's
"vendetta against Pete Rose." He sent a copy of the commissioner's letter to
Reuven Katz, Rose's attorney.

Giamatti had set a hearing date on Rose's case but postponed it once at
Rose's request. Before the commissioner could hear the case, however, Rose
sued in the Hamilton County state court in his hometown, Cincinnati, seeking an injunction against the commissioner. Rose asked Ohio state judge Norbert A. Nadel to halt the commissioner's proceeding.

Sitting in the Hamilton County Court of Common Pleas, Nadel listened to
testimony for two days on Rose's request for an injunction. Rose's attorneys
claimed the laudatory letter to Rubin about Peters, Rose's accuser, showed
that Giamatti was unfairly biased against the great ballplayer. Nadel, who was
required to stand for reelection in Cincinnati, granted Rose a temporary restraining order against the commissioner on the ground that Giamatti had
"prejudged" Rose's case. This was the first successful effort in the history of
baseball to interrupt, through litigation, a commissioner's investigation of alleged wrongdoing.

In response, the commissioner's office sought a more level playing field
than the state courts of Rose's hometown. It decided to seek to remove the
case to a more favorable setting—the federal court in Columbus, Ohio, a few
hours drive up Interstate 71 from the most loyal Reds fans. (Actually, Columbus is still "Reds Country." Cleveland Indians fans are sparse south of Can-
ton.) In arguing before the federal court, requesting that it take jurisdiction
in the case, the attorney for the commissioner said:

In the state court in Cincinnati, I need not describe Mr. Rose's standing. He is a local hero, perhaps the first citizen of Cincinnati. And Commissioner Giamatti is viewed suspiciously as a foreigner from New York, trapped in an ivory tower [his Yale connection], and accused of bias by Mr. Rose. Your Honor, this is a textbook example of why diversity jurisdiction was created in the federal courts and why it exists to this very day.

Because this suit was between citizens of different states, a federal court had the power to hear it under a grant of jurisdiction called "diversity jurisdiction." Using its power to remove a case from state to federal court, exercised when the plaintiff could have brought the case in federal court in the first instance, the trial court granted the commissioner's motion. Rose remained unrepentant, however, at least for the moment.

After intense negotiations, on August 23, 1989, the federal court case was settled when Pete Rose accepted permanent suspension from baseball. The public "Agreement and Resolution" between Rose and Giamatti related the history of the commissioner's investigation of Rose, concerning allegations that the manager and former star had "engaged in conduct not in the best interest of baseball in violation of Major League Rule 21, including, but not limited to, betting on Major League baseball games in connection with which he had a duty to perform" as the field manager of the Cincinnati Reds. Presumably to retract his earlier court claim that the commissioner's missive to Rubin suggested Giamatti was prejudiced in this matter, Rose acknowledged that the commissioner "has acted in good faith throughout the course of the investigation and proceedings." In exchange, the commissioner would make no formal finding on the betting allegations, but he was not prevented from making public statements relating to the matter.

As part of the delicate cotillion of language and deeds that accompanied the negotiated settlement, Rose agreed that the commissioner had the exclusive power to make a finding as to what acts were "not in the best interests of the national game of baseball." He waived any right to a hearing and accepted the commissioner's penalty:

a. Peter Edward Rose is hereby declared permanently ineligible in accordance with Major League Rule 15(c) and placed on the Ineligible List.

b. Nothing in this agreement shall deprive Peter Edward Rose of the rights under Major League Rule 15(c) to apply for reinstatement. Peter Edward Rose agrees not to challenge, appeal or otherwise contest the decision of, or the procedure employed by, the commissioner, or any future commissioner, in the evaluation of any application for reinstatement.

c. Nothing in this agreement shall be deemed either an admission or a denial by Peter Edward Rose of the allegation that he bet on any major league baseball game.

The commissioner had not yet extracted his full pound of flesh, however. In his prepared remarks announcing the settlement, reminiscent of Landis in his most effusive moments, Giamatti castigated Rose for this "sorry episode" and claimed that "one of the game's greatest players has engaged in a variety of acts which have stained the game." The former Yale pedagogue then waxed eloquent about "protecting the integrity of the game of baseball—that is, the game's authenticity, coherence and honesty":

> I believe baseball is a beautiful and exciting game, loved by millions—I among them—and I believe baseball is an important enduring American institution. It must ascend and aspire to the highest principles—of integrity, of professionalism, of performance, of fair play within its rules. It will come as no surprise that like any institution composed of human beings, this institution will not always fulfill its highest aspirations. I know of no earthly institution that does. But this one, because it is so much a part of our history as a people and because it has such a purchase on our national soul, has an obligation to the people for whom it is played—fans and the well-wishers in the millions—to strive for excellence in all things and to promote the highest ideals.

The Rose Litigation

Commentators on the Rose affair were quick to accuse Rose of having abused his "home court advantage." After all, what elected state court judge could rule against a hometown icon? The charge is groundless and unfair. The state court clearly had the power to hear Rose's action. Where else was Rose to bring his suit? In Manhattan, near the commissioner's office? In addition, the commissioner sought to have the action transferred to federal court in Columbus, a forum he found more suited to *his* interests. If Rose's choice of court can be criticized, the commissioner's attempt to have the matter removed to another court should be criticized as well.

On the merits of Rose's request to halt the commissioner's proceedings, many observers applauded the court's action in granting the injunction, reasoning that Giamatti had prejudged the facts in Rose's case. As a result, they said, Rose was denied the fairness of "due process." These comments also are misguided.

Rose was entitled to a hearing before the commissioner of baseball—the one already scheduled, which Rose sought to enjoin. Much like a criminal prosecutor, the commissioner of baseball must investigate allegations before even scheduling a hearing, to learn whether there is any substance to a charge. Finding Rose's accuser credible did not mean the commissioner had predetermined the ultimate outcome of the case. In fact, had the commissioner not found the accuser credible, he would have been unlikely to schedule any hearing. The hearing presented the accused Rose with the forum in which to offer his side of the story.

Rose's formal "due process" claims have no basis in the law. The Constitution protects "due process of law" in the Fifth Amendment. This obligation restricts actions only of instruments of government. (For example, parents do not need to afford their children due process of law before administering punishments.) Despite its self-proclaimed status as our "national" pastime, baseball is not a governmental entity. Without "state action," that is, action by some agency or body of government, Rose's rights to process were set forth in baseball's governing documents, not in the Constitution. The Major League Agreement and Rules guaranteed him a right to a hearing, and he was about to receive it when he ran to court.

Incidentally, Judge Norbert Nadel ran unopposed in the Republican primary for the Hamilton County Common Pleas Court and trounced Democrat Daniel Burke in the November 6, 1990, general election. Nadel said he did not think the Rose decision had an impact on his election.

Rose did not fair as well as Nadel. The commissioner of baseball banned him for life, which, we will see, also shut the doors of the Hall of Fame to him. On July 19, 1990, the federal district court sentenced Rose to five months in prison. Rose had pled guilty to tax evasion, primarily based on not reporting income received from selling autographs. When Rose reported to Marion

Federal Prison Camp in Illinois on August 8, 1990, they changed his jersey from famous retired number 14 to inmate number 01832061. Unfortunately for its competitors, Rose was now eligible to play on the Marion prison softball team, the Outlaws.

The Criminal, Civil, and Private Law Processes

Rose was not the only modern superstar to be accused of betting on games involving his own team. Giants manager John McGraw did it, and there is some evidence that Ty Cobb and Tris Speaker gambled as well. Rose was also not the only player or owner banned from baseball for a period of time for involvement in gambling or criminal activity. In fact, two stars on the postwar New York City baseball scene, Mickey Mantle and Willie Mays, were briefly suspended from baseball long after their retirement (and enshrinement in the Hall of Fame) because of their positions as spokesmen for Atlantic City gambling halls. The commissioner also suspended Yankees owner George Steinbrenner from baseball in 1990 for two years for consorting with gamblers.

Although Pete Rose's case was ultimately settled, it raises the question of the commissioner's power to conduct a hearing that could essentially "convict" Rose of gambling and "punish" him by declaring him ineligible and banning him from the game. The Constitution supplies procedural protections to an accused in a criminal action. However, Rose could not claim these protections because the commissioner acted under the Major League Agreement, not the criminal laws.

In Rose's case, the Major League Agreement gave the commissioner express authority to investigate allegations of gambling. Article 7, Section 3 of the agreement also states that all actions of the commissioner are recognized as taken "in the best interests of baseball." So, on its face, the Major League Agreement gives the commissioner far broader powers than those of a criminal court, and with fewer procedural protections for an accused party. However, the commissioner could not incarcerate Rose, only exclude him from the business of baseball.

Although the commissioner appears to have acted as a prosecutor, judge, and jury, Rose was never tried and convicted for the crime of gambling. The commissioner's actions were another example of private law application in a forum created by contract, not by public law. There are several essential distinctions between the two, often parallel legal systems.

Criminal law applies standards of conduct enacted by legislative bodies to prevent harm to society. Even if someone is injured by an act that violates a criminal law, it is society through the state that prosecutes, not the individual who was harmed. The aim of the prosecution is to punish the offender for his antisocial conduct, for harms done to the entire society. Generally, the state has significantly more power and resources than does a person accused of a crime. The Constitution limits how the state may exercise that power.

The Bill of Rights—the first ten amendments to the U.S. Constitution adopted by the first Congress—contains significant restrictions on the exercise of federal power. Additionally, the Fourteenth Amendment to the Constitution, enacted after the Civil War, extended most of those restrictions to the actions of state governments. The Constitution gives accused individuals a series of protections:

- the Fourth Amendment protection from unreasonable searches and seizures;
- the Fifth Amendment requirement of indictment before trial, protection against double jeopardy (being tried twice for the same blameworthy act), protection against self-incrimination (having to testify against yourself), and shelter against the deprivation of life, liberty, or property without due process of law;
- the Sixth Amendment guarantee to a speedy trial by jury, notice of the charges, the right to confront witnesses, and the right to assistance of a lawyer;
- the Eighth Amendment protection against cruel and unusual punishment.

State and federal rules of evidence and criminal procedure elaborate these essential constitutional protections.

None of these constitutional limitations applies to investigations or adjudications under a contract-created private law system, such as that operated by the commissioner of baseball. Despite general protestations over lack of "due process" and "constitutional rights," the internal, private law system applied by the commissioner operates free of constitutional restraints. The commissioner must act within the limits set by the enabling contract, the Major League Agreement.

One must assume, however, that the parties to the Major League Agreement would have expected that their commissioner, in carrying out the broad range of powers created by that agreement, would act in a fair manner in pursuit of the best interests of the game. Contractual "fairness" requires, at the very least, notice of allegations and an opportunity to respond to them. However, basic fairness does not require a full trial-type hearing, an independent decision maker, or proof beyond a reasonable doubt. Rose was entitled to fairness, and it appears he received it.

The formal criminal process of the state, designed to punish wrongdoers, must also be distinguished from the civil justice system. Civil law, based on dealings between private parties, provides a forum for the peaceful public resolution of private disputes. The injured party sues not to punish but to obtain personal redress for a violation of private interests. Consider a case where Able enters into a contract with Baker to build a house. Able then refuses to do the work. Able has not violated any criminal laws by breaching the contract, but Baker may sue Able for the damage suffered by his refusing to build the house, seeking, for example, the extra money that Baker had to pay another contractor to complete the house. Civil cases arising between individuals generally do not trigger the constitutional protections an accused has against the state in a criminal matter.

Civil and criminal trials, though they may use the same courtrooms and juries, differ substantially. To be convicted of a crime, a person must be proved guilty beyond a reasonable doubt. To receive compensation for a civil wrong, however, a plaintiff need only prove his or her case by a "preponderance of the evidence." Under our system of justice, we would rather allow some guilty parties to escape punishment than convict one innocent person of a crime he or she did not commit. Thus the government can fail to prove an accused person guilty, while a victim later can win a civil case against the same defendant based on the same evidence. For example, a defendant accused of murder and acquitted can subsequently be held liable for the tort of wrongful death.

The Rose contretemps shows well the distinctions among the criminal, civil, and private law systems. They all involve a form of adjudication, but they seek different goals by different means. Rose sought to move a private law dispute with the commissioner into the public law civil system; at the same time, prosecutors within the criminal law system investigated, accused, and convicted him of tax evasion. A consummate performer on the baseball diamond at third and at first base, Pete Rose was also a utility player in three different justice systems.

Baseball and Illegal Drugs

Although the threat to the integrity of the game posed by gambling ranks as the most serious peril faced by organized baseball, the sport has also had to address another societal vice, substance abuse, among its players. From the earliest days, ballplayers and saloons were synonymous, and many of the stars of the game were afflicted with alcoholism. In recent decades, however, as the U.S. government has targeted illegal drug use for special attention, organized baseball has discovered that its newly enriched athletes are as susceptible as other Americans to the lure of cocaine.

Major-league baseball first reacted to illegal drug use among the players in response to particular incidents, rather than in any comprehensive manner. In June 1980, authorities arrested Ferguson Jenkins, a stellar pitcher for the Texas Rangers, for possession of small amounts of cocaine and hashish. Commissioner Bowie Kuhn, exercising his authority to act in the best interests of baseball, suspended Jenkins until he either admitted or denied his guilt. Jenkins filed a grievance and challenged the commissioner's suspension in arbitration. The arbitrator overturned the commissioner's action, ruling that a suspension based only on Jenkins's arrest violated the essential American notion that he was "innocent until proven guilty." Moreover, he found that forcing Jenkins to admit or deny the charges before trial violated his constitutional right against self-incrimination. Kuhn's demand would "as a practical matter . . . jeopardize his [Jenkins's] defense in court."

The arbitrator's overall award was certainly correct: Kuhn was simply posturing for the media, and the arbitrator protected the player from the commissioner's overreaching. But his reasoning can be questioned. For one thing, an employer should have the right to remove an employee from the workplace when his presence would be disruptive. Kuhn could have made this point by demonstrating that the game's public image required that its players appear beyond reproach and free of accusations when it came to involvement with illegal drugs. But the commissioner failed to show that to be the case regarding Jenkins. Thus the suspension was questionable, not because the pitcher was "innocent until proven guilty" but rather because Kuhn had not demonstrated a legitimate business interest in removing him from the mound during the pendency of his case.

The arbitrator's invocation of a constitutional right was also misguided. The Constitution does not bind a commissioner, however much he may act as if his office were really a fourth branch of government—legislative, judicial, executive, and baseball commissioner. An employer, however, probably cannot discipline an employee for refusing to admit to having committed a crime away from the workplace. That would interfere with worker privacy, a right inherent in the employment relationship.

Commissioner Bowie Kuhn faced the next drug incident in August 1983, when three members of the Kansas City Royals club pled guilty to misdemeanor charges of "attempting to possess cocaine." Much to the surprise of the players, the U.S. magistrate judge did not place them on probation but instead sentenced them to three months in jail. The commissioner suspended the three players from baseball, an action upheld in arbitration. A fourth player, the Dodgers' Steve Howe, who had been with the Royals' players when they were arrested, was not convicted of a crime. Howe had a serious substance abuse problem, however, and had repeatedly failed drug tests administered by the major leagues. Kuhn issued Howe the first of what would be a series of suspensions from the game.

Shortly after these incidents, Bowie Kuhn was forced to address an incident involving Pascual Perez, an Atlanta Braves pitcher. Authorities arrested Perez in his native Dominican Republic for possession of cocaine with intent to distribute. Although convicted of the lesser charge of possession, he was imprisoned for three months by Dominican authorities. In response, the commissioner suspended him for one month. In this case, the penalty was overturned in arbitration. The arbitrator ruled there was "substantial question" of Perez's guilt and that Kuhn should not have relied exclusively on the Dominican justice system's finding of guilt.

Kuhn had better success with his suspension of Vida Blue, who had been convicted of cocaine possession in October 1983, served three months in jail, and paid a $5,000 fine. Kuhn prohibited the San Francisco Giants from signing Blue after his release from jail and suspended him for the remainder of the 1984 season, an action upheld in arbitration.

The national pastime seemed incapable of stemming the flood of bad press flowing from a few highly publicized incidents of player involvement with illegal drugs. This was the result, at least in part, of how the commissioner's office approached the issue. Cases were decided one at a time, widely reported by the media, and then followed by their inevitable review in arbitration. Baseball's private law system needed a uniform written policy to give notice to those covered that misconduct would result in sure, swift, and proportionate action. Baseball moved to such a policy, but success in addressing the scourge of drugs remained as elusive as a Hoyt Wilhelm knuckleball.

The Players Association and representatives of the owners worked quietly to address the growing public perception that drugs had infested the game. In the 1983 experimental Joint Drug Agreement, a pact that was far ahead of its time, the parties converted drug use from a disciplinary issue into a medical question. Three doctors—one selected by the union, the second by the owners, and the third by the two panel doctors—determined the facts of any particular case and applied preestablished treatment options.

September 1985 signaled the low point in baseball's war against drugs. The "Pittsburgh Drug Trials" centered on Curtis Strong, accused of selling cocaine to players. Testifying under a grant of immunity, baseball players detailed how drugs were purchased and distributed throughout the league. Although no players were convicted, Commissioner Peter Ueberroth "asked" those involved to submit to sanctions, and they "agreed." He also used this incident as a springboard to introduce a random drug-testing program for major-league players.

Ueberroth saw the drug issue as a matter of public relations for the industry rather than human relations with baseball's employees. He publicly tried to embarrass the Players Association into agreeing to random drug testing, something that had never been included in the Joint Drug Agreement. The commissioner announced a comprehensive drug-testing program that covered the umpires, personnel of his office and all the clubs, and minor-league ballplayers. The Players Association, however, rejected Ueberroth's program as applied to players at the major-league level. The union insisted that any testing scheme that could lead to discipline had to be negotiated with the union, rather than imposed unilaterally by the owners' commissioner. When Ueberroth ordered that individual player contracts contain a random testing requirement, the union grieved, claiming this was a matter for bargaining between management and labor. The union prevailed in arbitration.

Ueberroth then issued a revised "Baseball's Drug Policy and Prevention Program," abandoning random drug testing. This time the Players Association allowed the program to proceed without challenge. Commissioner Fay Vincent elaborated on the policy in 1991:

> Players are not subject to unannounced testing for illegal drugs. However, players who have admitted to illegal drug use, or who have been detected using illegal drugs, are subject to mandatory testing . . . for the balance of [their] professional career.

Shortly after that, when pitcher Steve Howe again ran afoul of the criminal law on cocaine possession, Vincent responded by banning him from baseball for life. Howe, however, grieved this "sentence," and the arbitrator found a lifetime ban too harsh because the commissioner's office had failed to give Howe the aftercare and drug-testing support it had promised. Howe finally left the game on June 22, 1996, after he was released by the New York Yankees. He had been suspended seven times for drug- or alcohol-related incidents.

Doc Gooden's Triumph and Tragedy

The successes and failures of Major League Baseball's drug-testing scheme are best illustrated by the career of one player, Dwight "Doc" Gooden. Gooden began his major-league career in 1984, two years after graduating from Hillsborough High School in Tampa, Florida. The New York Mets' first-round draft pick in 1982, Gooden's mastery on the mound quickly made him a modern legend. He struck out 276 batters in 1984, more than any other rookie in history, and won the Cy Young Award in 1985 as the best pitcher in the National League.

Shortly after winning Rookie of the Year in 1984, Gooden allegedly began using cocaine. By 1986, rumors spread that Gooden was a heavy user. He missed the ticker-tape parade down Broadway after the Mets 1986 World Series victory because of a hangover. Gooden tested positive for cocaine use during spring training the next year. He spent a month in rehabilitation and agreed to submit to follow-up random drug testing. But Gooden's career deteriorated, starting with an injury-plagued 1991 season. He was suspended for drug use again in 1994 and 1995.

In 1996, George Steinbrenner's New York Yankees offered Gooden (and fellow alleged substance offenders Steve Howe and Darryl Strawberry) a chance at redemption. On May 14, 1996, Gooden responded by throwing a no-hitter against the Seattle Mariners, his first in the major leagues. The triumph proved what a remarkable career Doc Gooden could have had, had he been drug-free for his entire career. It also displayed the failure of private ordering within the sport to address the very public drug issue.

We should not be surprised that the drug problem has proven intractable in professional sports. It remains a blight in all American communities and causes almost as much injury to society as alcohol abuse and cigarettes. Criminal actions related to the sale and use of illegal substances have overwhelmed the legal process, while drugs have corroded poor neighborhoods and aborted the lives of a generation. Although the media's clamor about drug use by baseball-player role models suggests its use is widespread, that is not likely. Most athletes appreciate that drugs can degrade performance over the long term.

Baseball's internal approach to substance use proceeded through a series of stages. At first, baseball ignored the issue, until it became a matter of public interest. The commissioner then applied discipline in an ad hoc manner, case by case, but each penalty was contested in arbitration. Finally, the commissioner's comprehensive program required the agreement (or at least the acquiescence) of the Players Association, a burdensome but essential step if any policy was to be successful.

Baseball's Hall of Fame

The ultimate recognition for a star baseball player is election to baseball's Hall of Fame. The Cooperstown shrine is an impressive monument to the game and its famed participants. What, then, should the deacons of this temple do with candidates who fall from grace as gamblers or substance abusers?

For those who fail to meet baseball's puritanical principles, the Hall may be an unattainable goal—even when one is the inimitable Pete Rose. Always playing the game with total abandon, Rose was caught stealing from baseball's mythic heritage. Banned from baseball for life, Pete Rose, the most prolific hitter of all time, has been excluded from the Hall of Fame.

The National Baseball Hall of Fame issued an "Official Statement" regarding Pete Rose, explaining his status. The rules for election to the Hall state: "Any player on Baseball's ineligible list shall not be a candidate for consideration by the Baseball Writers' Association of America (BBWAA) or the Baseball Hall of Fame Committee on Baseball Veterans" (the two bodies that elect members to the Hall). The announcement also explains how Rose can become eligible: "he must apply to the office of the Commissioner for reinstatement to Major League Baseball," be reinstated (the most difficult step), and then receive at least 75 percent of the ballots cast (the easiest step). The Hall of Fame board of directors denied any "vendetta" against Pete Rose:

> Nothing could be further from the truth. All of us at the Hall of Fame join the entire baseball community in conceding Pete Rose's impact on the game. How could any baseball fan not applaud the many accomplishments of the game's all-time leader in games played, at bats, hits and singles? The fact that over 15 Pete Rose artifacts are on exhibit in the [Hall of Fame] museum attests to our acknowledgment of the impact he has had on the game.

The facts suggest, however, that Rose's case has raised difficult issues for those who guard the sport's pantheon.

In 1992, the board of directors acted to alter eligibility requirements for election to the Hall of Fame, a move that affected Rose's case. It directly specified for the first time that a candidate must be on organized baseball's eligible list to stand for election to the Hall of Fame. The board of directors explained its decision to change the rules:

> Our decision has nothing whatsoever to do with the Hall of Fame's concern over how the writers might have voted in 1992 [with regard to Rose]. Very simply, our Board felt that it would be incongruous for anyone who has been declared ineligible by Baseball and therefore banned from the nation's ballparks, to still be eligible for Baseball's greatest honor. . . . The Hall of Fame has *every right* to establish the rules under which the voting process takes place. The BBWAA has

always conducted its balloting under the guidelines and ground rules set forth by the Hall of Fame.

Somewhat sheepishly, the board acknowledged that it was at fault for not adopting the rule a long time ago: "It should have been part of the Rules for Election since the first balloting took place in 1936. We are remiss for not having taken this action years ago." What if the baseball writers were to ignore the Hall's rules and vote to elect Pete Rose anyway? "We would obviously have to put together another group of electors."

Putting to one side the question of the merits of Rose's candidacy for the Hall of Fame, the commissioner's findings regarding his gambling, and his conviction for income tax evasion, the board of directors of the Hall of Fame seems to have inherited the hubris of the commissioner's office, best displayed for decades by Judge Landis: we make the rules; we change the rules; if the baseball writers do not follow what we say, we will create a new group of voters. We control baseball's shrine.

Participants in the game of baseball are subject to both public and private laws, administered by both public and private tribunals. This is not unique to baseball. We are all subject to various bodies of law. For example, we owe private responsibilities to our employers. If we fail to fulfill those obligations, we may be "banned" from that workplace after whatever process the employer provides. That action may spur a private lawsuit in civil court brought against the employer, claiming a wrongful discharge; or it may result in a grievance, if we work under a collective bargaining agreement. If we are fired for theft or for taking an ax to our supervisor, we may also be subject to the public criminal process. Unlike Pete Rose and other ballplayers who have run afoul of the laws of baseball, however, most of us will not have to worry about our eligibility for election to the Hall of Fame.

This marks the beginning of a true renaissance and golden era for the game. ACTING COMMISSIONER BUD SELIG

9: Baseball's Labor Wars of the 1990s

SONIA SOTOMAYOR

Born to immigrant parents in the projects of the South Bronx, a short walk from Yankee Stadium, federal judge Sonia Sotomayor was drafted to play the pivotal role in resolving the great baseball labor wars of the 1990s. When the National Labor Relations Board filed suit seeking an injunction against the club owners, the court clerk's office selected Judge Sotomayor at random to preside over the case that would save the baseball business from self-destruction. *(Photo courtesy of Judge Sonia Sotomayor)*

Perhaps it was inevitable that during the mid-1990s, baseball's opposing forces of management and labor would converge for still another confrontation. The owners had always possessed the economic power to reject player demands. They lacked only the solidarity to resist the Players Association's repeatedly successful efforts at the bargaining table to reallocate industry resources. Although the owners had achieved a victory in the 1985 negotiations by increasing the eligibility period for salary arbitration from two to three years, overall, management's performance in the labor wars rivaled that of the 1899 Cleveland Spiders, who finished the season with 20 wins and 134 losses.

The owners were determined to change their dismal record in 1994. The resulting labor dispute lasted almost three years and risked the future of the national pastime. It would grow to involve a federal administrative agency, a federal court, a federal mediator, and the president of the United States. Bill Veeck, the great maverick club owner, once said that "baseball must be a great game, because the owners haven't been able to kill it." The 1994–1996 period would be the greatest test of Veeck's aphorism.

The legal text for the baseball labor wars of the 1990s was the National Labor Relations Act. That federal statute required management and labor to bargain in "good faith" over "terms and conditions" of employment. The meaning of those two phrases would be pivotal in establishing the conditions under which labor and management could resolve their bargaining dispute.

The surprising hero in this battle of the 1990s was not a player, an owner, or a union official. In April 1995, federal district court judge Sonia Sotomayor, at the behest of the general counsel of the National Labor Relations Board, stepped up to the plate to enforce the national labor law principle of good faith bargaining. Sotomayor bats ninth on our Baseball Law All-Star Team. For now, she has had the final say.

The Business of Baseball

Baseball franchises are intertwined with corporate America. Most clubs are owned by corporations or large groups of wealthy individuals who earned their fortunes outside the baseball enterprise. Some observers rue the loss of the individual baseball entrepreneur, but few owners ever earned their living from baseball. William Hulbert, the founder of the National League, was a Chicago coal baron long before he brought his organizational genius to the national game. For some, baseball simply has provided a valuable opportunity to promote their outside business; witness Gussie Busch's linkage of the St. Louis Cardinals to his beer empire or the Atlanta Braves' role as programming fodder for Ted Turner's television superstation. In fact, about half the baseball franchises are now owned either by a media company or by the team's principal commercial broadcast sponsor. The remainder are organized as sole proprietorships or partnerships.

Baseball management periodically bemoans the financial hardship suffered by club owners. Under the owners' calculations, most teams report book losses. But others see diamonds where the magnates claim only sand. The demand for baseball franchises and their selling prices have exploded at the same time that player salaries have skyrocketed. Basic economics instructs us that a business expected to lose money each year cannot be sold, although it is possible that purchasers are speculating or motivated by prestige, civil pride, or the love of the national pastime. Nonetheless, the record shows a dramatic escalation in sale prices, more than might be justified by nonmonetary reasons. The Baltimore Orioles were sold for $12 million in 1979, for $70 million in 1989, and again for $173 million in 1993, when the franchise had the good fortune to be able to play in the publicly funded superstadium at Camden Yards. The Seattle Mariners were sold for $13 million in 1981, for $89.5 million in 1988, and again for $106 million in 1992. Despite the owners' protestations, baseball is a profitable business when measured by return on investment. But while purchase prices of franchises have increased geometrically, not all franchises are of equal value. There are "haves" and "have-nots" within the baseball family of franchises. This proved to be one cause of the disastrous labor dispute of the 1990s.

Even "losses" in the accounting books can be seen as an economic benefit. Bill Veeck was the first owner to claim his players' contracts for tax purposes as an "asset" of the team, which could, therefore, be depreciated as a tax deduction, typically over a five-year period. Under current tax rules—they seem to change almost annually—club owners may deduct half a franchise's purchase price from taxable income. If the tax deductions exceed the profits from baseball, an owner can apply the excesses against profits in other enterprises.

A great source of profit to baseball franchises flows from league-enforced territorial exclusivity. Clubs do not have to compete for fan attention and attendance, and the gate constitutes about 50 percent of a team's revenue. A team may own or lease its stadium and earn profits from the lease of luxury boxes or from the latest entrepreneurial device, marketing "permanent seat licenses" that permit holders to purchase tickets for these seats in the future. To varying degrees, clubs also earn revenue from contracts with food and parking concessionaires. The market value of the different territories varies greatly: a franchise in Pittsburgh does not have the same earning potential as one of the New York City franchises.

Broadcast revenues, both national and local, and trademark concessions make up a considerable share of a club's profits. National television revenues, estimated at $15 million per team in 1993 but reduced sharply under the 1994 contract, are distributed equally, as are the profits from major-league licensing contracts with product manufacturers. Clubs do not share local broadcasting revenues, however, and these can vary greatly, depending on the size of the local television and radio markets.

Unlike the revenue-sharing system used by other professional sports, visiting clubs in baseball receive only a small portion of the home gate—20 percent in the American League and about 5 percent in the National League. As we will see, it was the revenue disparity among clubs that was said to be the origin of the labor strife in the 1990s, although some think the extended dispute was simply a case of management's dogged determination to recapture preeminence in the enterprise, instead of sharing that status with the Players Association.

From 1903 until the 1960s there were sixteen baseball franchises, eight in each circuit. The number first rose to twenty-two in 1961, twenty-four in

1962, then to twenty-six in 1977, and to twenty-eight in 1993. In 1998, two new franchises raise the total to thirty. Every new franchise must pay sizable fees to join the cartel, an amount then shared among the owners. The two new entries in 1993, Miami and Denver, paid $95 million each for the privilege of entering the league. The Tampa and Phoenix franchises, the 1998 additions, are paying close to $150 million each to join the major leagues.

The Business of the Players Association

As a fraternal organization of baseball players during the 1950s and early 1960s, the Major League Baseball Players Association had posed little challenge to the club owners. After all, the owners supplied the capital that made the professional game possible and even supplied funding for the Players Association. It never dawned on most players that there might be something inequitable in the system or that anything needed changing. But after the appointment of Marvin Miller as executive director, as we have seen, everything changed, including the players' self-image. The union turned baseball into a money machine for the players, and in the process, the baseball enterprise evolved into a modern entertainment business, no longer simply a summertime diversion. Baseball lost its innocence, which always had been part of its charm.

Players Association's coffers have profited from its successes. The union is now a multimillion-dollar business in its own right. Compared with the clubs, however, the union bureaucracy remains lean (and, the owners would probably add, "mean"). Four experienced lawyers lead the organization: Executive Director and General Counsel Donald Fehr, Associate General Counsel Gene Orza, and Assistant General Counsels Lauren Rich and Michael Weiner. Fehr has two special assistants, former major-league ballplayers Mark Belanger and Don Bernazard, who proved invaluable during the labor wars of the 1990s. With support from attorneys Doyle Pryor, Bob Lenaghan, and, periodically, agent Steve Fehr, the Players Association has become the strongest trade union in the country.

Players on each club elect a player representative, and these representatives meet twice annually as the union's executive board. One player from each league is selected as the league player representative—in effect, the president of the union for that circuit. Between meetings, the subcommittee of the executive board governs the union. Members of the union pay dues to the organization in an amount proportionate to the length of their major-league service. Currently, members pay twenty dollars a day for every day of major-league service, an amount deducted by their clubs from players' paychecks and forwarded to the union.

Union revenues have come a long way from the bottle-cap agreement Marvin Miller signed with Coca-Cola to supply the union with its first source of independent income. The Players Association manages the substantial licensing revenues received from baseball card companies, computer games, and clothing, which total about $90 million a year. The union terms this revenue "special dues," and it is then distributed to the players by formal action of the executive committee. The individual player's share of the licensing revenue is proportionate to his major-league service.

Management's Strategy

In June 1990, when asked about future labor negotiations, Commissioner Fay Vincent told *Baseball America,* "I think it would be romantic and somewhat silly to assure you or the American public that there isn't going to be confrontation the next time around. The history tells you that there will be." Little did Vincent realize (at least publicly) that he would be the first casualty in that confrontation.

In preparation for their penultimate contest with the Players Association, the owners decided to eliminate any possibility that the commissioner of baseball might interfere with their plans or actions. The public viewed the commissioner's office as a neutral force in the enterprise, and at times the commissioner has been known to act independently. That was a risk the owners could not afford to take as they prepared for the next set of negotiations with the Players Association. The owners knew the commissioner served at their pleasure. Attorney Fay Vincent, the incumbent of the office, did not have Peter Ueberroth's leadership acumen or Bart Giamatti's intellectual charm. The gods of baseball would sacrifice Vincent before the battle would begin. The owners fired their commissioner in September 1992, clearing the labor relations playing field of any possible interference from his office.

Instead of searching for a new commissioner—any commissioner could be an impediment—on September 10, 1992, the owners appointed their well-liked colleague, Bud Selig, the owner of the Milwaukee Brewers, as acting commissioner. He vowed to stay in the "temporary" role only until a new deal was struck with the union. (In a 1997 case unrelated to the labor dispute, a federal district court in New York upheld Selig's claim that he had never legally been elected or appointed acting commissioner. Rather, he served only as chairman of baseball's executive council. Nonetheless, everyone called Selig the Acting Commissioner, and so will we.) The owners were now ready for a showdown at the bargaining table.

The parties' 1990 collective bargaining agreement expired on December 31, 1993. The owners decided they would insist on restructuring the baseball enterprise in order to maintain its profitability. They had tried the same approach in 1990 but then quickly aborted their effort. This time, the owners stuck by their plan with remarkable tenacity.

Baseball's profit situation was of greatest concern to the owners of small-market franchises, such as Bud Selig. As acting commissioner, Selig convened a meeting of baseball owners in Fort Lauderdale to discuss sharing the substantial revenue generated by the entire baseball enterprise among all club owners. Alone among the major sports, baseball had a tradition of club financial independence. Visiting teams shared modestly in home gate receipts; they pooled only the proceeds of national television contracts; and teams in major markets, such as George Steinbrenner's New York Yankees, received substantial payments for local television rights to their game while clubs in minor markets received only modest returns.

Under lucrative local television contracts, big-market teams sold the rights to televise both home and away contests. Under the copyright laws, however, rights to a "performance" belong to the home team. How could Steinbrenner sell to the MSG network and WPIX in New York City the right to televise a Yankees-Brewers game in Milwaukee County Stadium? That required the consent of the Brewers, the home team.

Baseball club owners had long been party to agreements under which home teams gave permission to visiting teams to televise contests to the visiting team's television market. The agreements expired in 1993, and the small-market teams used these arrangements as a convenient hostage, demanding a greater share of total baseball revenue in exchange for renewal of these understandings. At the owners' Fort Lauderdale meeting in January 1994, the owners agreed to continue the television arrangements under a new revenue-sharing formula. There was only one significant condition: the players would have to agree to a salary cap that would limit each club's total player costs. Baseball owners thought the salary cap had saved professional basketball from bankruptcy and that it would be the salvation of baseball as well. The rich club owners would share with the poor club owners a portion of the money saved when they paid their players lower salaries. The strategy was brilliant: the players would pay for the revenue sharing.

The Salary Cap

The salary cap concept had been the brainchild of National Basketball Association (NBA) commissioner David Stern and the late union leader Larry Fleisher. By the early 1980s, two-thirds of NBA franchises were losing money. Some individual owners, most notably Ted Stepien of the Cleveland Cavaliers, had spent wildly on free agents, and player salaries had skyrocketed beyond the financial capability of most franchises. The NBA's national television contract produced only modest revenues for each club, and basketball arenas, even if sold out for every contest, had limited capacity that could not cover team payrolls.

Under the 1983 salary cap, basketball management and the players shared the industry's revenue and limited each club's aggregate player salaries. They calculated the cap by taking 53 percent of the NBA's total "defined gross revenue" (gate receipts and proceeds from sale of national broadcast rights), less payments made to the players' benefit funds, divided by the number of teams in the league. That became the team ceiling, a presumptive maximum total salary. Those teams whose payrolls already exceeded the cap were allowed to phase it in over time. The arrangement also provided a guaranteed team minimum aggregate salary, calculated by subtracting the aggregate total dollar expenditures by teams above the leaguewide ceiling from 53 percent of the total revenue, then dividing that number by the number of teams. Each team was required to spend at least that amount on its total-team player salaries.

The salary cap was complex, almost medieval, in operation. Exceptions to the team cap allowed a club to re-sign its own free agent even if that placed the club above the cap. A club could replace a retired or waived player at half his salary if the team was already over the cap. Teams could also replace a traded player with another player at no greater than 100 percent of the salary last paid the traded player.

Basketball's salary cap had more holes in it than a Green Bay Packer cheese-head hat, and teams quickly learned how to avoid its constraints. The most significant loophole allowed a team to exceed its cap to re-sign its own free agent. General managers would sign a player for one year at a low salary to fit within the cap and then re-sign the player with a substantial salary increase, free from cap control, after he declared free agency.

Revisions in the basketball salary cap during the 1995 negotiations closed some loopholes but opened still others. Under the current collective bargaining agreement, teams can no longer sign a free agent for one year at a low salary, only to recapture him the next year at an exorbitant salary. Only a free agent who has been under contract to a team for at least three years can be re-signed for any salary amount, free from the salary cap. A free agent with a club for two years or less can be re-signed only for the leaguewide average player's salary or for a 75 percent raise over his prior year's salary, whichever is greater. In addition, all teams over the cap can sign one or more free agents for a total of up to $1 million, notwithstanding the cap. Finally, the new agreement allowed a team to exceed the salary cap to sign its first-round draft pick under the terms of the new rookie wage scale contained in the collective bargaining agreement.

These exceptions and others made the NBA's soft salary cap more of a suggestion than a mandate. For example, the 1996–1997 Chicago Bulls team salary was $58 million when the leaguewide team cap was calculated at $24.3 million. Admittedly, Michael Jordan's salary of $30.14 million skewed the Bulls' payroll.

Most commentators have concluded that the NBA's cap was modestly successful. It stopped the league's financial hemorrhaging and fostered a cooperative spirit between the owners and players, who became "partners" in the enterprise. Much of its success must be attributed to Stern and Fleisher, two of the great modern leaders in professional sports. The commissioner's office in the NBA became a powerful entrepreneurial force. By comparison, the club owners in Major League Baseball decided to suspend the operation of their commissioner's office before negotiations began.

Baseball owners found the salary cap system attractive for many reasons. It set a club's total salary exposure for a season. It did not matter what the club paid individual players, since the total payroll remained under control. The cap also offered management a powerful weapon during individual negotiations with agents representing players below the superstar level. The club could state, with the backing of the negotiated salary cap, that legally it could not pay the player what he wanted. Owners thought the cap would return baseball to the turn of the twentieth century, when Phillies owner Colonel John I. Rogers told Napoleon Lajoie he could not pay the ballplayer more than the established leaguewide salary limit.

Negotiations Begin

The negotiations between representatives of the baseball club owners and the players commenced in Tampa in March 1994. These early discussions made little progress. On May 23, the owners' Player Relations Committee representative Richard Ravitch, a New York City lawyer, proposed some minor adjustments to the now-expired agreement—eliminating termination pay, trade demands, and major-league service credit for players called up from the minors in September. The owners' core proposal on compensation came three weeks later.

On June 14, the owners' representative proposed a salary cap. Players would receive half the industry's revenue (substantially less than they were receiving under the expired contract), and team payrolls would be limited to 84 to 110 percent of the average team payroll. The proposal abolished salary arbitration and lowered free agency eligibility from six years of service to four. Free agents with less than six years' service would be restricted, however. A club could match any rival club's offer and keep its player.

About a month later, the union rejected management's bold departure from the free market system of individually bargained salaries. The union proposed instead that the owners lower service eligibility requirements for salary arbitration to two years, where it had been before 1985; eliminate the contract restriction on repeat free agency within five years; and raise the contract minimum salary to $175,000. It took management only a little over a week to reject this counterproposal.

Such early maneuvering is commonplace in collective bargaining negotiations. Much of the posturing about initial positions is announced (or leaked) to the media, which often takes these positions seriously. No one should have really expected either party to accept its opponent's demands at this stage, primarily because there was no compelling reason to do so, and at this early stage, it was unclear what each party really wanted from negotiations. The "subjective utility functions," a party's true positions (discussed in Chapter 4), had not yet been revealed.

The Strike

On July 28, 1994, the Players Association set August 12 as a strike deadline. Scheduling the strike near the end of the regular season maximized its potential impact. Half the owners' revenue comes from fan attendance, and the gate peaks in late August and early September. In addition, most management revenue from national television contracts results from World Series telecasts. The union timed its strike to place the greatest economic pressure on the clubs.

Withholding services is the one concrete economic weapon unionized employees have under national law, but, as we saw in Chapter 4, a strike creates significant costs for both parties. Although management can no longer rely on the strikers' services, employees are not paid during a strike. Even threatening a strike is not cost-free. It can cost the union its credibility at the bargaining table. And a union can never be sure its members will be willing to take this collective step; it is one thing to threaten and quite another to carry out the strike.

Management must evaluate a union's threat to strike in terms of its potential impact on the entire business enterprise. In the manufacturing sector, for example, management may be able to replace strikers or stockpile goods for shipment during a strike. In the service sector—the commercial amusement of baseball falls into that category—services cannot be stockpiled. A game (or season) not played is a revenue opportunity lost forever. But all is not lost for management when a service workers' union strikes. The strike reduces costs dramatically because management does not pay the strikers—not an insignificant consideration when your average employee earns a million dollars a season.

Perhaps to demonstrate that the players' strike threat would not intimidate them, the club owners failed to make the payment to the players' pension fund in August, in apparent violation of national labor law. During negotiations, even after the expiration of the collective bargaining agreement, management must maintain the status quo regarding compensation and benefits until it bargains to impasse. The club owners claimed they were not required to make the fund payment after the expiration of the collective bargaining agreement, relying on a waiver provision in the pension document that they said freed them from responsibility. Nonetheless, the Players Association filed an unfair labor practice charge with the National Labor Relations Board, which later found merit to the union's allegation.

Although the parties continued to meet periodically at the bargaining table, all reports suggest that little real bargaining went on, and they made little progress. At the strike deadline, the union ordered a walkout—the eighth job action in the industry in little more than two decades. Although management had never really believed that high-priced ballplayers would strike, the players had done so repeatedly in response to management's failure to accede to their demands. Once again in 1994, the ballplayers walked out together and stayed out for what would be the longest strike in professional sports history.

After a union calls a strike, it normally takes the parties some time to evaluate its effectiveness. The baseball economic battle of 1994–1995 would be no blitzkrieg but rather trench warfare, based on the economic staying power of the parties and the potential impact of public opinion. By timing its strike strategically to impose the greatest amount of cost on the owners, the union sought to convince management to abandon its salary cap proposal and renew the existing free agency system. Surely, thought the players, the owners could not afford to complete the season without the World Series.

The Players Association underestimated the owners' resolve. The well-timed strike strategy failed when, on September 14, 1994, Acting Commissioner Bud Selig canceled the remainder of the season, including the World Series. Management would not allow the union to control the schedule of this economic battle.

The fans' hopes for a quick end to the dispute faded as their disgust increased at the players' and owners' stubbornness. For the first time since 1904, when John Brush, the owner of the New York Giants, disdainfully rejected postseason play against the Boston champions of the American League, there would be no fall classic. Baseball's fortunes—and its popularity with the public—dropped to its nadir.

Under national labor law, the owners did not need the union's agreement to restructure the business of baseball. While its assent would have been preferable, no one on management's side was naive enough to think the Players Association would accede to a dramatic shift in resources and influence away from the players. Only twenty years earlier, the *Messersmith* arbitration decision had opened the free agent market to competitive bidders. The union would not relinquish this hard-fought victory without a major fight.

The clubs were required to participate in good faith negotiations to the point of impasse, when national law allowed management unilaterally to implement its last offer to the union. Recognizing that the union was unlikely to agree voluntarily to their fundamental restructuring proposal, management understood from the outset that unilateral implementation would be the only way things would change in the baseball business. If they were going to "save baseball," they would have to be unyielding.

Again, as in prior work stoppages, the fans were left out of the equation. Although they pay the freight, either directly at the stadium turnstiles or indirectly by patronizing baseball's commercial sponsors, fans do not have a seat at the bargaining table. National labor policy is based on the premise that the adversarial relationship between labor and management will produce agreements that serve the public's interest by achieving labor peace. The assumption is that if products or services become too expensive as a result of a costly agreement, the market response will inform management and labor how to adjust their relationship in the future or lose their customers forever. This provided little solace to the fans, who had been enjoying the wonderful baseball season of 1994, with numerous players on record-breaking paces and exciting pennant races underway.

In a few labor disputes, the public's interest in resolving the conflict may be represented at the negotiating table by the presence of a federal mediator. The parties to a dispute may request the assistance of a mediator, or, in rare cases, the government can decide that the public interest requires mediation. The 1994 baseball strike was a high-profile event, especially for President Bill Clinton, whose party had just suffered a disastrous congressional election defeat that brought, for the first time in more than a generation, Republican control to both houses of Congress.

Mediation must be distinguished from arbitration or any other process that results in an authoritative adjudication of disputed issues. A mediator supervises negotiations. He or she cannot impose a settlement; rather, the mediator helps the parties try to reach a settlement. No mediator can single-handedly bring about an agreement, without a commitment by the parties involved. A mediator often paces the negotiations by controlling when parties should meet face to face. A good mediator may devise novel formulations on thorny issues that allow the parties to move toward agreement. Using a full range of constructive interpersonal skills, a mediator cajoles the parties toward a zone where both sides find more utility in settlement than in conflict. An experienced mediator also knows when to throw a tantrum and when to threaten to quit. When both parties eventually realize that they are better off settling than fighting, they will reach an accord. Sometimes they reach a settlement merely to get the mediator out of their hair.

After consulting with Labor Secretary Robert Reich, President Clinton appointed former secretary of labor William J. Usery to mediate the baseball dispute. Usery had an excellent record of successfully resolving intractable labor disputes. But by all accounts, Usery, although appointed with much fanfare, met his match in these warring parties. On December 14, the talks broke down. The next day, the owners announced they would give the negotiations another week before declaring an impasse and unilaterally implementing their salary cap plan.

On December 22, the Players Association presented the owners with its plan to ease the revenue disparity among club owners. It proposed a luxury tax on those teams with payrolls that dramatically exceeded the major-league average. Under the union's system, there would be a 10 percent tax on clubs' payrolls that exceeded the league's average by 30 percent. Now there were two different approaches on the bargaining table: a salary cap, with a lid on a club's total player payroll, and a luxury tax, which would make exorbitant player salaries even more expensive and thus less likely to be negotiated. It was not likely that the Players Association thought its plan would be accepted, but it wanted to keep the negotiation process going so the clubs could not declare an impasse in negotiations. Management did not even respond to the Player Association's proposal.

The next day, December 23, the owners cut the Gordian knot: they declared that an impasse existed in negotiation and unilaterally implemented their salary cap proposal. Later analysis showed that the owners' new salary system would have reduced total player salaries and benefits by 11 percent. On December 27, the union filed another unfair labor practice charge with the Labor Board, claiming the owners' action was an illegal unilateral change in terms and conditions of employment.

It was not sufficient for the owners simply to impose a new labor relations system. They needed to prepare for a baseball season without the regular players. The strike had already cost the clubs hundreds of millions of dollars in lost revenue and jeopardized whatever goodwill remained in the public's heart (and pocketbooks) for the national pastime. During January 1995, the owners decided to proceed with the next phase of their plan: replacement baseball. Clubs signed minor leaguers and retired players to fill team rosters for the coming season. They readied their spring training facilities to receive these men, who would serve as pawns in the ongoing labor relations chess game. Some of these replacement players (the union, of course, called them "scabs") saw this as their one chance to play in the major leagues. Others who had left the game dreamed of revisiting past glory on the diamond. Few potential future stars of the game jumped at the opportunity, but the clubs (with the sole exception of Baltimore Orioles owner Peter Angelos, who was a union labor lawyer) prepared to resuscitate the sport on their terms.

On January 26, 1995, President Clinton ordered mediator Bill Usery to bring both sides back to the bargaining table and announce a deadline for a settlement. When the talks resumed on February 1, the owners abruptly abandoned their salary cap concept and proposed a 75 percent luxury tax on payrolls between $35 and $42 million and a 100 percent tax on payrolls over $42 million. Two days later, after the owners learned that the Labor Board was prepared to issue an unfair labor practice complaint alleging that management had illegally implemented the salary cap, the owners rescinded their December plan and switched tactics. The owners now revoked the authority of individual clubs to sign player contracts and eliminated salary arbitration and the anticollusion clause that had proved so troublesome to management.

On February 5, Usery announced that if the parties were not able to agree on their own, he would propose the terms of a settlement to President Clinton the next day. On February 7, in an extraordinary move, unprecedented in professional sports, Clinton called both sides in the baseball labor dispute to the White House and personally attempted to mediate a settlement. Usery's proposal to the president had recommended a 50 percent tax on club payrolls over $40 million, much closer to the owners' position than to the players'. Instead of seeking agreement on this settlement—the president must have been advised that the Players Association would find Usery's plan unacceptable—Clinton asked both sides to accept binding arbitration of their differences. Under Clinton's plan, the parties would present their positions on a new contract to a respected neutral, who would decide what the terms of the new collective bargaining agreement would be. The union agreed, but the owners refused. The next day, the Players Association filed new unfair labor charges with the Labor Board, protesting the owners' latest unilateral changes in the terms of the collective bargaining agreement.

Talks took a three-week hiatus as the parties reassessed their positions. When negotiations resumed in Scottsdale, Arizona, the union boosted its tax proposal rates and lowered the thresholds for payment, but they remained far below a level acceptable to management. It became obvious that the parties would not soon reach an agreement at the bargaining table. The parties' representatives were not even resolving minor issues effectively, often a preliminary step to agreement on major differences. In fact, little real negotiation was going on. The epic struggle was heading nowhere in the direction of resolution.

The Labor Board Intervenes

When labor negotiations stall, one of the parties must do something to alter the status quo if a settlement is to occur. Management broke what it had considered an impasse in negotiations in December 1994, by implementing its salary cap proposal, and the Players Association responded by filing an unfair labor practice charge with the Labor Board, claiming that management had violated its bargaining obligation under federal law. The agency found merit in this claim, but management avoided further proceedings by revoking its salary cap plan.

Management then altered the status quo again by unilaterally implementing further changes; it revoked the authority of individual clubs to sign contracts, eliminated salary arbitration, and abolished the anticollusion clause. The Labor Board investigated the union's unfair labor practice charge contesting management's actions, in order to decide whether the allegations warranted issuing a formal complaint against the clubs. Such a complaint would then be tried before an administrative law judge (ALJ). In such cases, the Labor Board reviews the ALJ's decision and the board's decision may be appealed to the federal appellate court. In some rare cases, the Labor Board can decide to shortcut this multiyear process and, under Section 10(j) of the National Labor Relations Act, seek injunctive relief directly in federal court to restore the status quo.

There could not have been a more propitious time in history to bring a sports labor law issue to the National Labor Relations Board. The chairman of the Labor Board, appointed by Clinton, was Stanford Law School professor William Gould, one of the nation's foremost experts in both labor and sports law. On March 26, 1995, Gould convened a rare Sunday meeting of the five members of the Labor Board. Labor Board general counsel Fred Feinstein requested that the board seek a Section 10(j) injunction against the baseball owners, and the Labor Board agreed. The next day, Feinstein, through his regional director in New York City, filed for a federal court injunction to restore the status quo that had existed before management made its February 6 changes to the labor relations system. The parties to the suit were the regional director of the Labor Board and the Major League Baseball Player Relations Committee (representing the owners in negotiations with the union), and the Players Association intervened and participated in the action.

At the end of March 1995, while the Labor Board's case against the owners was pending in court, the owners formally voted to begin the baseball season with replacement players, following the strategy that had proved so successful in 1987 for the National Football League, when it crushed its players' union. The era of "replacement baseball" was about to begin.

Thus the Labor Board, the owners, and the Players Association made their way to the courtroom of our final All-Star, Judge Sonia Maria Sotomayor. Born to immigrant parents in the projects of the South Bronx, a short walk from Yankee Stadium, Judge Sotomayor was the first member of her family to attend college. A summa cum laude graduate of Princeton University and

Yale Law School, she had worked as an assistant district attorney in New York as a criminal prosecutor. She then moved to civil practice as a partner in a New York firm, before her appointment to the federal bench by President George Bush in 1992. She served for twelve years on the board of directors of the Puerto Rican Legal Defense and Education Fund.

After she was nominated as the first Latina federal district court judge in the nation's largest city, Sotomayor told the Senate Judiciary Committee at her confirmation hearing that she believed "those of us who have opportunities in this life must give back to those who have less. It is never easy to encourage others to do the same, but I do think it is important for public figures, for legal educators, for the bar to constantly and repeatedly encourage public service."

Nothing in her personal history foretold that she would be drafted to play the pivotal role in resolving the great baseball labor war of the 1990s. In fact, the baseball dispute was Sotomayor's first labor case, either as a judge or as a lawyer. When the regional director of the Labor Board filed the suit seeking injunctive relief, the court clerk's office selected Judge Sotomayor at random to preside over the case.

In court, the parties presented evidence about the baseball negotiations. The court action focused on the owners' February edict that had prohibited clubs from negotiating with individual players, abolished salary arbitration, and eliminated the anticollusion provisions of the expired agreement. Management argued to Judge Sotomayor that the Labor Act did not require the owners to negotiate with the union over these subjects. If it need not negotiate over these matters, then its action could not violate the law.

Mandatory Subjects of Bargaining

The National Labor Relations Act requires management to negotiate over "wages, hours, terms and conditions of employment." As interpreted by both the Labor Board and by the courts, this phrase covers some, but not all, topics about which the union may want to negotiate. The Labor Board distinguishes between what it has termed "mandatory" and "permissive" subjects of bargaining. Management must bargain over mandatory subjects, such as wage rates and the hours of work, and may bargain over permissive subjects.

A union cannot compel management to bargain over permissive subjects if management refuses to do so.

What, then, are permissive subjects? Examples from various board and court decisions identify some principles to be applied in making the determination. Management need not bargain with the union over "the design of the product" a company manufactures. In the baseball context, this might be analogous to a management decision to give a batter four strikes instead of three (during the early years of the game, fouled pitches were not counted as strikes and for one year, in 1887, a batter actually had four strikes) or to set the length of a game at seven, rather than nine, innings. Matters that lie "at the core of entrepreneurial control" are management decisions and constitute permissive subjects for bargaining. A union may not legally strike to compel management to accede to its position on a permissive subject of bargaining.

Classifying a subject as mandatory or permissive is very important under national labor law, but it is not an easy task. Must management bargain over the installation of artificial turf on a baseball playing field? The field could be seen as the functional equivalent of the industrial work floor. Because issues of worker safety have always been held mandatory subjects, it is likely that the decision to install artificial turf would fall into the mandatory category. Management may decide, as it often has during the history of the game, to raise or lower the height of the pitcher's mound. Lowering the mound increases the batter's chance of success and, in turn, the run production of a team, certainly an aspect of the "design of the product." Changing the height of the mound, however, may give pitchers sore arms and shoulders. An aspect of the game that directly affects playing conditions is likely a mandatory subject.

Even if a topic is a mandatory subject of bargaining, this does not give a union veto power over management's decision. Classification as a mandatory subject merely means that, on request, management must bargain in good faith with the union over the issue. It need not concede or change its course. After good faith bargaining to an impasse, management may put its decision into effect without the union's agreement.

Even if the union cannot demand bargaining about management's decision because it is a permissive subject, "at the core of entrepreneurial control," it can demand that management bargain about the *effects* the decision might have on the employees. Management might decide to eliminate the designated hitter rule in the American League, but it would have to bargain with the union about the impact of that decision on those players in the American League whose continued employment depends on that rule. Even regarding effects bargaining, management need not obtain a union's permission before carrying out a change in operations, if it has bargained in good faith to impasse about those effects.

The Court's Decision

Under the National Labor Relations Act and prevailing court precedent, Judge Sotomayor had to decide whether the Labor Board had proved there was "reasonable cause to believe" that baseball management had violated the Labor Act. In making that determination, courts defer in some degree to the expertise of the Labor Board. Often, the toughest hurdle in seeking an injunction is satisfying the element of irreparable injury. The board has to prove that without an injunction the employees will be irreparably injured. Baseball players have short playing careers—on average, about five years—and thus, without an injunction, some of these young men would lose the opportunity to play in the major leagues before the Labor Board and appeals court could rule on the unfair labor practice complaint. The court also considered the need to restore the status quo that had existed before the alleged violation to protect the integrity of the Labor Board's processes and the public interest in collective bargaining. The judge concluded that the Labor Board had shown irreparable injury.

Turning to the merits, Sotomayor explained that all parts of what she called baseball's "reserve/free agency" system related to the wages the players earned and thus were mandatory subjects of bargaining. One part of management's contested action prohibited individual clubs from negotiating with individual players. That change had a direct impact on wages. As such, the judge concluded, it was a mandatory subject, and therefore management could not unilaterally implement the change without bargaining to an impasse with the union.

The legal analysis of the owners' suspension of the anticollusion restriction contained in the expired collective bargaining agreement was more difficult. The clubs argued that the clause unreasonably limited the owners' right to bargain collectively under the Labor Act. They needed to be able to "collude" to prepare effectively for negotiations. Sotomayor responded in her opinion that the Labor Act protected only the *employees'* rights to act collectively, not the *employers'*. There is no such thing as an "employer union." Once again, the court held that the anticollusion protection was a mandatory subject as a significant part of the parties' reserve/free agency system.

Concerning management's abolition of salary arbitration, the owners argued that this unique baseball system set new terms of employment for players and thus was beyond the scope of mandatory subjects of bargaining. In the private sector, negotiations settle most contracts, but a few parties resort to an outside, neutral arbitrator to set the terms of their new contracts, when they are unable to agree on their own. The Labor Board previously had ruled that this so-called interest arbitration was a permissive subject of bargaining and that a union could not insist on bargaining over whether a provision calling for interest arbitration will be part of a new agreement. The club owners argued that salary arbitration was much the same.

Judge Sotomayor disagreed, finding that salary arbitration did not create future contractual obligations. Under the salary arbitration procedure, there was no question that the players were going to provide services to the club; salary arbitration was simply the method for assigning dollar figures as compensation. Salary arbitration did not create new contracts, only old contracts with dollar amounts based on stated and negotiated contract criteria. It really was not very different from a system in specialized industry that set wages within the agreement's term, based on the salary paid other workers in that industry, or that adjusted wages according to the consumer price index. In any case, stated the judge, even if salary arbitration was analogous to interest arbitration, it was so intertwined with the setting of wages that it also was a mandatory subject of bargaining.

Judge Sotomayor issued the injunction that the Labor Board requested and ordered the owners and the players back to the bargaining table. How long were they now required to bargain? They were ordered to negotiate, in good faith, until one of three things occurred: (1) they reached an agreement; (2) the Labor Board issued a final order on the union's underlying unfair labor practice allegations; or (3) the parties reached a true impasse after good faith bargaining. Although the court did not order the players to "play ball," the union offered to do so, and management accepted. Against all odds, the 1995 season began on April 26, only a few days late.

The Parties Reach an Accord

Although the federal court injunction cleared the negotiating table, cluttered by management's unilateral changes and the union's modest tax proposals, the parties were not yet ready to renew their efforts at reaching agreement. The 1995 and 1996 baseball seasons proceeded as scheduled, but the negotiations accomplished little for more than a year. The judicial order did not mandate immediate bargaining, and it took time to heal the wounds on both sides of the table. Months passed without direct contact between the representatives of the club owners and the players.

The return to the table came quietly, with lower-level discussions designed to build trust between the parties. The parties did not announce these private meetings to the press, and they occurred in out-of-the-way sites. Acting Commissioner Bud Selig and Executive Director Donald Fehr were not ready to come to the table. Much of the bargaining for the Players Association was done by Lauren Rich, the third in command at the Players Association for many years and the most influential woman in the professional sports business. Rich was a savvy negotiator, coming to the Players Association after years working for the National Labor Relations Board and the International Ladies' Garment Workers Union.

During 1996, the owners again changed their negotiators, hiring Randy Levine, the personable labor commissioner for New York City, to try again to reach an accord. Levine followed Richard Ravitch and Charles O'Connor as the owners' chief spokesperson at the table. Perhaps because of the new personality at the table or simply because of the mere passage of time, the parties finally seized the opportunity to end the longest labor dispute in professional sports history.

Meeting throughout the summer of 1996, with an especially productive set of sessions on the August 9–11 weekend, and well into the fall of that same year, Levine for management and Fehr for the union hammered out a delicate compromise that called for revenue sharing among the clubs, with a luxury tax on a club's total salary and a payroll tax on the players. On October 24,

1996, while the New York Yankees and Atlanta Braves were battling in a marvelous World Series, the negotiators reached a tentative agreement. What must have seemed like "the Hundred Years War" was almost over—but it would not end without one last spasm. The players had voted to authorize their representative to reach an agreement, and union negotiators believed Levine had the same authority. Apparently, he did not.

On November 6, 1996, the owners voted eighteen to twelve (including the two future expansion teams as voting members) to reject the proposed contract, repudiating the agreement their negotiator had reached. They instructed Bud Selig to seek additional "improvements" from the union.

The owners made one more unsuccessful attempt to wring more concessions out of the union. For the first time in more than a year, owners and players came face-to-face at the bargaining table. Although the union had always included players in its bargaining team, after March 1995 management's lawyers had negotiated without their clients present. Despite the presence of owners, however, there was no real negotiating to do, because the union would not budge from the tentative pact. A deal was a deal.

Although there was some discussion in the press about National League owners seeking a revote on the tentative agreement, something more was required before the owners would switch their position on the pact. It was ironic that the final straw was supplied by Chicago White Sox owner Jerry Reinsdorf, said to be the chief opponent of the tentative agreement and a constant proponent of owner restraint in salary payments. Shortly after the vote rejecting the agreement, Reinsdorf signed Cleveland Indians power-hitting left fielder Albert Belle to a five-year, $55 million free agent contract, making Belle the highest-paid player in the sport. The hypocrisy was unprecedented, even for the baseball magnates. One week later, on November 26, 1996, in Reinsdorf's hometown of Chicago, the owners voted twenty-six to four to approve the new collective bargaining agreement without any changes. Reinsdorf voted against the agreement. After forty-seven months and the loss of more than a billion dollars to the players and the owners, there was labor peace in the baseball industry.

To the bitter end, the owners continued to seek further concessions from the union. Although the negotiated pact provided for a one-year experiment in interleague play, when they ratified the agreement the owners insisted that this be stretched to a second season. On December 5, the union agreed.

The New Agreement

The new collective bargaining agreement will revolutionize the business of baseball, although it will take some time to measure the full scope of its impact. The agreement, retroactive for the 1996 season, runs through October 31, 2000, and the union has the option of extending it for another year. Of greatest interest to baseball fans, and for the first time ever, American and National League clubs began regular season interleague play in 1997.

The new agreement addresses financial imbalances within the leagues. The richest clubs will share local revenues with the poorest clubs, allocated under a complex formula. Starting with the 1997 season, a maximum of five teams with payrolls exceeding a set amount—$51 million in 1997, $55 million in 1998, $58.9 million in 1999—will pay a "tax," of 35 percent in 1997 and 1998 and 34 percent in 1999; and that tax will be used, in part, to fund a revenue-sharing pool. Players will also contribute to this revenue-sharing pool, paying a tax of 2.5 percent on their 1996 and 1997 salaries, with money coming from licensing income and other revenue sources.

The revenue-sharing concept first embodied in the owners' Fort Lauderdale agreement had been transmuted during negotiations. Article 25 (B)(5) of the new agreement defines the objectives of the revenue-sharing plan:

> A principal objective of the revenue sharing plan is to promote the growth of the Game and the industry on an individual Club and on an aggregate basis. Accordingly, net receipts and Supplemental Pool Payments received under the revenue sharing plan will be used in furtherance of this objective. . . .The Clubs and the Association agree that the amounts paid as Supplemental Pool Payments are contributed on behalf of the members of the Association . . . to further the growth and development of the Game with the view toward advancing the interest of both the Clubs and the Players.

Thus the primary stated purpose of revenue sharing was not for the rich to pay the poor; rather, the concept was intended to "grow the game." In addition, the parties established an Industry Growth Fund (IGF) "to promote the growth of baseball in the United States and Canada, as well as throughout the world." A seven-member board of directors—three selected by the owners and three by the union and one "independent" member appointed jointly by the parties—oversees the operations and activities of the fund. The IGF will be amply funded by the luxury and payroll taxes.

Even the salary arbitration system is adjusted in the new agreement: instead of one arbitrator deciding salary arbitration disputes, three-arbitrator panels will hear half the cases in 1998, 75 percent of the cases in 1999, and all the cases in 2000. Eligibility for salary arbitration, the process followed, and the criteria arbitrators use remain unchanged.

Perhaps the most fascinating provision in the new agreement, and one that would bring the history of the business of baseball full circle, requires labor and management jointly to request that Congress repeal baseball's *Federal Baseball* antitrust exemption as it applies to labor relations. Article 28 of the agreement states:

> The Clubs and the Association will jointly request and cooperate in lobbying the Congress to pass a law that will clarify that Major League Baseball Players are covered under the antitrust laws (i.e., that Major League Players will have the same rights under the antitrust laws as do other professional athletes, e.g., football and basketball players), along with a provision that makes it clear that the passage of that bill does not change the application of the antitrust laws in any other context or with respect to any other person or entity.

As the seventy-fifth anniversary of Holmes's ignoble opinion, 1997 seemed an appropriate occasion for the repeal. Finally, baseball would join all other professional team sports under the aegis of national law.

Although it is premature to determine a "winner" or a "loser" in the labor struggles of the 1990s—and perhaps both sides lost—we can reach some preliminary conclusions about the process and the participants. For the first time, club owners demonstrated the same level of solidarity as the players showed. How did management unify as never before? It likely was the result of group dynamics. The club owners had great personal loyalty to Bud Selig, their well-liked colleague. Selig had learned a great deal by watching how the Players Association maintained cohesiveness within its diverse organization. During the labor wars of the mid-1990s, Selig constantly "worked the phones," consulting with fellow owners and informing them of bargaining developments. Owners also participated in bargaining sessions until March 1995. Face-to-face with player activists, often in very tense bargaining sessions, the owners became personally "invested" in the process. The group dynamic within management's camp was different this time, and Selig deserves the credit for keep management unified.

The labor war also proved the mettle of the Players Association during the worst of times. Unlike many other professional sports unions, the Players Association remained an organization governed by the rank and file through their elected player representatives. American League player representative David Cone and National League player representative Tom Glavine attended every meeting, as did other union stalwarts, including Brett Butler, Jay Bell, Terry Steinbach, and B. J. Surhoff. The union kept the player agents informed and involved in the bargaining process. Team conference calls from the union's offices on Forty-Eighth Street in New York City were common. As part of "crisis management," even the union's support staff worked around the clock.

The turning point in negotiations was management's agreement to explore a luxury tax in lieu of a salary cap. Having botched the implementation of the salary cap under national labor law, the owners were willing to listen to the union's strategy. The salary cap would have *prohibited* clubs from spending more than a set amount; the luxury tax, by contrast, would *inhibit* clubs from spending, imposing a brake on the market. Will the agreement's new arrangement affect player salaries? Both parties acknowledge that it will, but only experience under the new system will determine the extent of the restraint.

Union research established that each year only eight to ten clubs were active in the free agent market. Under the new agreement, the luxury tax is paid by a maximum of five teams, leaving three to five clubs still uninhibited in the free agent market. The union's economists predict that this will be sufficient competition to keep the bidding process alive.

Denouement

The 1990s labor wars illustrate many of the business themes and legal processes discussed throughout this book. The major leagues, a commercial business structure that is the product of private ordering among club owners, determined in the 1990s to exert private economic pressure to recapture power and profits lost to the Major League Baseball Players Association in earlier bargaining and arbitration confrontations. To prepare for the fray, club owners rewrote their own internal rules and practices by dismissing their commissioner of baseball and, for the first time since they created the office in the early 1920s, not replacing him. (The Commissioner's Office remained in operation under the able leadership of Brewers' owner Bud Selig, who served in an "acting" capacity.) They then privately devised a unique method for sharing revenues among the clubs in their Fort Lauderdale agreement, a system altered slightly in further meetings among the owners. When presented with the owners' demands, the Players Association responded with its own private economic pressure, calling a strike that lasted 234 days—the longest in baseball history.

Although begun as a purely private affair, the parties' dispute quickly involved public processes and institutions, both formal and informal. The union filed three sets of unfair labor practice charges with the National Labor Relations Board, claiming the owners had engaged in bad faith bargaining under national law. The federal government intervened, appointing a mediator and even drafting the president of the United States into a failed attempt to resolve the dispute. Finally, Chairman William Gould and the National Labor Relations Board initiated the federal court action under federal labor law that brought about a truce in the economic wars, returned the game to the field, and, eventually, induced the negotiators to return to the bargaining table. After the owners finally approved the settlement on November 26, 1996 (as chance would have it, Gould learned that news from me during a telephone conversation on another matter), Gould issued a press release lauding the agency's role in establishing a "level playing field" for collective bargaining, "a prime example" of the Labor Board's successful use of its authority to seek injunctive relief. He concluded, "I am especially pleased that the result here is a collective bargaining agreement in the sport that is America's and my favorite pastime. Today's agreement is indeed a long deep drive for collective bargaining." Although equally deserving of praise, Judge Sonia Sotomayor did not issue a press release.

On March 14, 1997, representatives of the baseball club owners and the players finally signed their new basic agreement. Acting Commissioner Bud Selig said, "This marks the beginning of a true renaissance and golden era for the game." Executive Director Don Fehr said only that the parties had endured "arduous negotiations." Private ordering at its most sophisticated level—the new complex collective bargaining agreement that remade the business of baseball—ended the long and almost terminal labor dispute.

If you come to a fork in the road,

take it. YOGI BERRA

Conclusion

Yankees catcher Lawrence Peter "Yogi" Berra is famous for his platitudinous maxims, most of which contain kernels of insight hidden within the twisted verbiage. "It ain't over until it's over" is, perhaps, the most famous Yogi-ism, and nothing could better characterize the state of the legal process as it interacts with the business of baseball. It ain't over yet, and even then it won't be over.

The baseball enterprise entered a new era with the 1996 collective bargaining agreement, but the contours of the future of the business remain unclear. Labor and management reached an accommodation only when pragmatism combined with exhaustion. Their new charter will allow the sport to market its commercial amusement globally and offer the opportunity for the game to recapture the attention (and affection) of the fans of the game. But the new cooperative structure does not ensure success for the enterprise or the people involved in it. As Yogi might have said, "They still have to play the game to find out if anyone will come and watch."

The End of the Antitrust Exemption

A clause in the new collective bargaining agreement provides that the parties will jointly seek congressional modification of the antitrust exemption. Although this provision is symbolically important, it should not have any practical effect. In 1996 the Supreme Court restrained the use of the antitrust laws in the sports labor relations context, in a case involving the 1989 negotiations between the National Football League (NFL) Players Association and football management. Franchise owners had proposed establishing "developmental squads" of practice and replacement players, whom they would pay a flat $1,000 a week, but the union rejected the fixed salary. After the parties reached an impasse in negotiations, management unilaterally implemented its proposal. The union sued, claiming the clubs' concerted action in setting salaries "restrained trade" and violated the antitrust laws.

Without a union, an agreement between competing firms on worker salaries would violate the antitrust laws. In the labor context, however, a court must balance procompetitive antitrust policies with the equally important policies supporting collective bargaining. None of the federal statutes tells the court how to reconcile these competing policies. The Supreme Court had ruled, however, that the parties to a collective bargaining agreement enjoy an "implied" labor exemption to the antitrust laws for anticompetitive policies that are adopted as part of the collective bargaining process. Had the union agreed to management's proposal on pay for the development squads, for example, the resulting pact would have been immune from antitrust liability. But the NFL imposed its development-squad pay policy at a bargaining impasse; it was not the consensual product of collective bargaining. Management acted unilaterally after negotiations failed. Should the antitrust exemption apply in that situation?

In 1995, the District of Columbia Circuit Court of Appeals said the antitrust exemption still applied. Chief Judge Harry Edwards, a former labor law professor at the University of Michigan Law School, ruled that the implied antitrust exemption continued beyond impasse in negotiations, if the union remained a viable entity. The exemption even covered terms unilaterally imposed by management. Management must still bargain in good faith to impasse, and if it did not, the Labor Board could find an unfair labor practice. In any case, the antitrust laws had no effect if the union continued to represent players for purposes of collective bargaining. Under Edwards's ruling, a union had two options to use in opposing management's actions: it could exercise its economic power by striking, or it could cease to represent the players by seeking its own decertification by the Labor Board. If the union were defunct, the players could sue under the antitrust laws. The Supreme Court endorsed Edwards's approach and affirmed the circuit court's judgment.

Thus congressional internment of *Federal Baseball* would not affect the power of the Major League Baseball Players Association at the bargaining table in any material manner. The union could not threaten an antitrust court action without also deciding to end its status as the bargaining representative for the players, the suicidal strategy that the NFL Players Association actually followed in 1987.

There is some faint hope that the 1996 agreement will usher in an era of cooperative relations in the baseball business. Indeed, the very act of a joint request to Congress might bode well for the future relationship between the parties. Negotiators schooled in war for years, however, may have real trouble implementing a labor peace. Building mutual respect and trust will require a miracle rivaling the 1969 Mets.

Other Issues

Although we have addressed many significant legal issues in the history of the development of the baseball industry, some others warrant passing mention. They are likely to require additional attention in the years to come.

INTELLECTUAL PROPERTY

One of the most profitable aspects of the baseball business has nothing to do with action on the diamond. The players and the clubs maintain property interests in their likenesses, statistics, and logos; exploiting those interests is a multimillion-dollar business. Baseball cards existed as early as the 1880s, when they were sold with chewing tobacco. Today, rare cards sell for hundreds of thousands of dollars, considerably more than the players depicted on the cards ever dreamed they could earn from playing the game.

As baseball goes global, trademark, copyright, and other intellectual property issues will proliferate. Even disputes about the use of names and logos of defunct teams—for example, the Brooklyn Dodgers—will regularly find their way to court for resolution.

EMINENT DOMAIN AND FRANCHISE FREE AGENCY

In an era of "franchise free agency," sports teams move from town to town, much as the itinerant Cincinnati Red Stockings did during their triumphant 1869 tour. This time the teams do not seek competition but rather compensation in the form of new stadia and better deals. Starting in 1953, with the sale of the St. Louis Browns to a Baltimore group that renamed the franchise the Orioles and with the Boston Braves move to Milwaukee (and, thirteen years later, to Atlanta), club owners have enjoyed the free marketplace. The real gold rush began in 1957, when the Brooklyn Dodgers and the New York Giants deserted Gotham for the West Coast. Lured by virgin markets and sweet deals, club owners crisscrossed the country. Others used the leverage of a threatened move to extract more public funds from the hometown government.

What does the future hold for the movement of franchises? The expansion of organized baseball into Florida, Arizona, and the Rocky Mountains through the creation of new franchises did not end the owners' wanderlust. The Carolinas have seen new franchises in football, basketball, and hockey. They would certainly welcome a baseball club. Nashville pines for recognition as a major-league city. As demographics change and the population shifts, new cities will enter the competition for a club of their own. What can a local government do to obtain control over a franchise, to keep it from moving?

Oakland, California, tried to use its power of "eminent domain" to keep its fabled football team, the Raiders, from leaving town. Although it had some initial success under California state law, the legal strategy ultimately failed. Of course, Al Davis's Raiders now have returned to Oakland, tired of the bright lights of southern California and the empty seats of Los Angeles Coliseum. Courts have long held that the power of eminent domain extends beyond tangible assets and physical property. We may see, in baseball's future, a test of whether the power of eminent domain extends to a sports franchise.

GENDER EQUITY

The next barrier to be broken in professional sports is the inclusion of female athletes on previously all-male teams. Women already play a prominent role in tennis, golf, figure skating, and basketball. Women jockeys and race-car drivers led the way, and there have been women professional hockey goalies at the minor-league level. Women reporters enter men's locker rooms and announce sports contests on television. Why would we not think that women will play baseball at the major-league level?

Globalization and Beyond

Participants in the business of baseball now have the opportunity to plan the future scope of their enterprise, especially if the 1996 collective bargaining agreement fosters a true labor-management partnership. One of the most exciting prospects lies in the internationalization of the sport of baseball. Other professional sports are globalized, led by the enormous success and popularity of soccer's World Cup and the quadrennial Olympics. Tennis and golf tours span the world, and the best athletes from all countries now participate in professional basketball and hockey leagues.

In 1996, the New York Mets and the San Diego Padres played the first U.S. regular-season major-league baseball game ever held in Mexico, long a hotbed of interest in the sport. Their visit to Mexico was occasioned by the Republican presidential convention in San Diego. The reception they received bodes well for future expansion southward. Within the next decade, new or relocated franchises should spring up in Latin America. The next major markets are Europe and the Pacific Rim. Baseball has seen the future; now it can prepare to meet it. It has come to a fork in the road and, to use Yogi's advice, it has decided to take it.

A key theme of this book on the baseball business and the legal process has been the overall balance between the individual interests of players and the institutional interests of the clubs and their owners, with the public interest sitting uncertainly in the background. We have watched cycles of dominance by the clubs or leagues on the one hand and the countervailing power of the players union on the other. Although we may wish for a harmonious and just relationship within the enterprise, the legal process has been used by the participants to achieve their partisan goals, rather than serving as an instrument of stability and fairness.

The challenge to those who despair at the current state of the national pastime is to conceptualize a framework to move toward equilibrium. Peeling away the mythology, we find a game played by very rich young men who make other rich men even richer. Yet the emotional pull of the sport is unmistakable. How, then, can we distinguish between the fraudulent and the legitimate claims of the participants? Do any of them seek anything beyond more money? Before we dismiss this inquiry as unimportant when applied to a summertime diversion, remember that the entertainment industry is a worldwide leviathan. Its regulation should be an important subject in an ongoing public policy debate.

Baseball's future is linked inextricably to the legal process. We can foresee continued use of private methods of dispute resolution, private ordering of relationships by contract, and the occasional involvement of formal institutions of government, such as the courts and federal agencies. As baseball goes global, however, there will be additional legal processes at work—for example, international trade and copyright agreements—and involvement of the world agencies that administer those compacts. Finally, the worldwide technological revolution will affect the business of baseball in ways not easily foretold. We can rest assured, however, that law and lawyers will come along on the global run around the bases.

Notes

INTRODUCTION

America and baseball have always been inextricably intertwined. Jacques Barzun's famous quote is frequently cited: "Whoever wants to know the heart and mind of America had better learn baseball" (*God's County and Mine: A Declaration of Love Spiced with a Few Harsh Words* [Boston: Little Brown, 1954]).

Roger Angell is baseball's finest storyteller. His lyric prose relates the poetry of America's Game. For example, in *Season Ticket* (Boston: Houghton Mifflin Co., 1988), Angell wrote:

> Baseball is not life itself, although the resemblance keeps coming up. It's probably a good idea to keep the two sorted out, but old fans, if they're anything like me, can't help noticing how cunningly our game replicates the larger schedule, with its beguiling April optimism; the cheerful roughhouse of June; the grinding, serious, unending (surely) business of midsummer; the September settling of accounts, when hopes must be traded in for philosophies or brave smiles; and then the abrupt sunning-down of autumn, when we wish for—almost demand—a prolonged and glittering final adventure before the curtain.

His love for the sport does not cloud his vision, however. He wrote in *Five Seasons* (New York: Simon and Schuster, 1977), "We have begun to understand at last that baseball is most of all an enormous and cold-blooded corporate enterprise."

Dozens of law schools now offer a course or seminar in sports law. In the last decade, excellent casebooks have been written by Paul Weiler and Gary Roberts, *Sports and the Law* (Westbury, N.Y.: Foundation Press, 1993), and Ray Yasser, James Mc-

Curdy, and C. Peter Gopelrud, *Sports Law Cases and Materials,* 3d ed. (Cincinnati: Anderson Publishing Co., 1997). The comprehensive treatise by John Weistart and Cym Lowell, *The Law of Sports* (Charlottesville, Va.: Michie Co., 1979), although out of date, remains the best supplementary work in the field. There are a few superb law review articles in the field, including the classic work by Bob Berry and Bill Gould, "A Long Deep Drive to Collective Bargaining: Of Players, Owners, Brawls, and Strikes," *Case Western Reserve Law Review* 31 (1981): 685.

A wonderful online source of baseball information on the worldwide web can be found at http://www.sabr.org, the home page of the Society of American Baseball Research.

CHAPTER ONE

Henry Hart and Albert Sacks first presented a course in the legal process to classes at the Harvard Law School in the 1950s. For decades, students read photocopied course materials, collected as "tentative editions." I was privileged to take the course from Professor Sacks in 1968. Westbury, New York's Foundation Press published the ageless materials as *The Legal Process: Basic Problems in the Making and Application of Law* in 1994, after the deaths of these two great legal scholars.

The Monte Ward case is reported at *Metropolitan Exhibition Co. v Ward,* 9 NYS 779 (NY Sup Ct 1890).

Harold Seymour is the definitive chronicler of baseball history. Seymour tells the story of the Brotherhood and the Players League in chapter 19 of his *Baseball: The Early Years* (New York: Oxford University Press, 1960). Albert Spalding offers a decidedly different version in *America's National Game* (New York: American Sports Publishing Co., 1911).

The history of the American labor movement can be found in John Dunlop and Derek Bok, *Labor and the American Community* (New York: Simon and Schuster, 1970), and in Edwin Beal, Edward Wickersham, and Philip Kienast, *The Practice of Collective Bargaining* (Homewood, Ill.: Richard D. Irwin, 1976), among other sources.

CHAPTER TWO

Nap Lajoie's case is reported at *Philadelphia Ball Club, Ltd. v Lajoie,* 202 Pa 210, 51 A 973 (1902).

After Lajoie left the Cleveland franchise and returned to Philadelphia, the readership of the local newspaper recommended renaming the club the Indians, in honor of Lewis M. Sockalexis, a Native American who played for the Cleveland Spiders from 1897 until 1899. The origin of "Chief Wahoo," the present-day Indians' racially offensive logo, is unknown.

E. Allan Farnsworth's treatise on the law of contracts, *Contracts*, 2d ed. (Boston: Little Brown, 1990), explains the legal and theoretical bases for the enforcement of consensual exchanges.

CHAPTER THREE

Oliver Wendell Holmes's opinion is reported at *Federal Baseball Club of Baltimore, Inc. v National League of Professional Clubs*, 259 U.S. 200 (1922). The Supreme Court's *per curiam* opinion is at *Toolson v New York Yankees*, 346 U.S. 356 (1953). Justice Harry Blackmun's opinion in Curt Flood's case is reported at *Flood v Kuhn*, 407 U.S. 258 (1972). Robert Woodward and Scott Armstrong relate the behind-the-scenes interplay among the Supreme Court justices in the Flood case in *The Brethren* (New York: Simon and Schuster, 1979).

There are many treatises available on antitrust law, but its application to baseball is best told by John Weistart and Cym Lowell, *The Law of Sports* (Charlottesville, Va.: Michie Co., 1979), 480–89.

Dean Cowen's analysis of *Federal Baseball* appears in "Baseball and the Law—Yesterday and Today," *Virginia Law Review* 32 (1946): 1164.

CHAPTER FOUR

Marvin Miller's autobiography, *A Whole Different Ball Game* (New York: Birch Lane Press, 1991), is generally considered a reliable, although partisan, retelling of the story of the revitalization of the Major League Baseball Players Association. The history of baseball's labor-management struggles of the 1970s is well told in Lee Lowenfish and Tony Lupien, *The Imperfect Diamond* (New York: Stein and Day, 1980).

The Practice of Collective Bargaining (Homewood, Ill.: Richard D. Irwin, 1976), by Edwin Beal, Edward Wickersham, and Philip Kienast, remains the essential text on labor-management relations. Further, I have described baseball's salary arbitration process in Roger Abrams, "Sports Labor Relations: The Arbitrator's Turn at Bat," *Entertainment and Sports Law Journal* 5 (1988): 1.

CHAPTER FIVE

Branch Rickey's battle with Kenesaw Mountain Landis over the farm system is told by Ted White in chapter 2 of his *Creating the National Pastime* (Princeton, N.J.: Princeton University Press, 1996); by Lee Lowenfish and Tony Lupien in *The Imperfect Diamond;* and by Harold Seymour in chapter 20 of his *Baseball: The Golden Age* (New York: Oxford University Press, 1971).

The Jackie Robinson story is told, among other places, in Geoffrey C. Ward and Ken

Burns, *Baseball: An Illustrated History* (New York: Alfred A. Knopf, 1994), and in Joel Zoss and John Bowman, *Diamonds in the Rough* (Chicago: Contemporary Books, 1996). It has also been related in many 1997 newspaper accounts celebrating the fiftieth anniversary of Robinson's entry into major-league play, a pivotal event in baseball history.

A detailed account of the Catfish Hunter arbitration has not been published, but the arbitration opinion is available from the offices of the Major League Baseball Players Association. In *Five Seasons,* Roger Angell wrote, "Considerable evidence suggests that the A's were united and matured most of all by their shared individual resistance to the Finley style and the Finley presence." Charles Finley's unsuccessful suit against Commissioner Bowie Kuhn is reported at *Charles O. Finley & Co. v Kuhn,* 569 F2d 527 (7th Cir 1977), *cert. denied* 439 U.S. 876 (1978).

CHAPTER SIX

Arbitrator Peter Seitz's award in the Messersmith grievance arbitration has been published by the U.S. Bureau of National Affairs as *In the Matter Comprising Twelve Clubs of the National League of Professional Baseball Clubs and Twelve Clubs Comprising the American League of Professional Baseball Clubs, Los Angeles and Montreal Clubs and Major League Baseball Players Association,* in volume 66 of the Labor Arbitration Reports (Washington, D.C.: U.S. Bureau of National Affairs, 1975), at page 101. The Eight Circuit's enforcement of the award appears as *Kansas City Royals v Players Association,* 532 F2d 615 (1976). The best text on the labor arbitration process overall remains Frank Elkouri and Edna Elkouri, *How Arbitration Works,* 4th ed. (Washington, D.C.: Bureau of National Affairs, 1985).

The "Steelworkers Trilogy" is reported as *United Steelworkers v American Mfg. Co.,* 363 U.S. 564 (1960); *United Steelworkers v Warrior & Gulf Navigation Co.,* 363 U.S. 574 (1960); and *United Steelworkers v Enterprise Wheel & Car Corp.,* 363 U.S. 593 (1960).

The economic impact of free agency is discussed in Andrew S. Zimbalist, *Baseball and Billions* (New York: Basic Books, 1992), chapter 4; and in Paul M. Sommers, *Diamonds Are Forever: The Business of Baseball* (Washington, D.C.: The Brookings Institution, 1992).

CHAPTER SEVEN

The collusion arbitration cases have not been published but are available through the offices of the Major League Baseball Players Association. Arbitration technicalities are discussed in Owen Fairweather, *Practice and Procedure in Labor Arbitration,* 2d ed. (Washington, D.C.: U.S. Bureau of National Affairs, 1983).

CHAPTER EIGHT

The story of Pete Rose's fall from grace is based on numerous newspaper accounts. The court decision, *Rose v Giamatti*, no. A8905178 (Ohio Ct CP, Hamilton County, June 25, 1989), is available on LEXIS and WESTLAW. The Hall of Fame's statement on Rose can be found at http://www.enews.com/bas_hall_fame/members/ rosestate.html.

The definitive work on the Black Sox scandal is Eliot Asinof's *Eight Men Out* (New York: Holt, Rinehart, and Winston, 1963).

CHAPTER NINE

The discussion of the labor wars of the 1990s is based on numerous contemporary newspaper accounts and conversations with some of the participants. In particular, I found the 1994–1996 reporting by Murray Chass of the *New York Times* to be both accurate and insightful. Jack Sands and Peter Gammons, *Coming Apart at the Seams* (New York: Macmillan Publishing Co., 1993), was also most helpful. Judge Sonia Sotomayor's opinion, marking "the beginning of the end" of the long dispute, is reported at *Silverman v Major League Baseball*, 880 FSupp 246 (1995).

Although more than two decades old, Robert Gorman's *Basic Text on Labor Law* (St. Paul, Minn.: West Publishing Co., 1976) remains the foremost primer on the Labor Board and court decisions under the National Labor Relations Act.

Bibliography

Angell, Roger. *Five Seasons.* New York: Simon and Schuster, 1977.

———. *Late Innings.* New York: Simon and Schuster, 1982.

———. *Season Ticket.* Boston: Houghton Mifflin Co., 1988.

Asinof, Eliot. *Eight Men Out.* New York: Holt, Rinehart, and Winston, 1963.

Barzun, Jacques. *God's Country and Mine: A Declaration of Love Spiced with a Few Harsh Words.* Boston: Little Brown and Co., 1954.

The Baseball Encyclopedia. 9th ed. New York: Macmillan Publishing Co., 1993.

Baseball's Hall of Fame, Cooperstown: Where the Legends Live Forever. New York: Arlington House, 1988.

Baseball's Hall of Fame Fiftieth Anniversary Book. New York: Prentice Hall Press, 1988.

Beal, Edwin, Edward Wickersham, and Philip Kienast. *The Practice of Collective Bargaining.* Homewood, Ill.: Richard D. Irwin, 1976.

Bok, Derek C., and John T. Dunlop. *Labor and the American Community.* New York: Simon and Schuster, 1970.

De Tocqueville, Alexis. *Democracy in America.* New York: Oxford University Press, 1947.

Dickson, Paul. *The Dickson Baseball Dictionary.* New York: Facts on File, 1989.

Elkouri, Frank, and Edna Elkouri. *How Arbitration Works.* 4th ed. Washington, D.C.: Bureau of National Affairs, 1985.

Fairweather, Owen. *Practice and Procedure in Labor Arbitration.* 2nd ed. Washington, D.C.: Bureau of National Affairs, 1983.

Farnsworth, E. Allan. *Contracts.* 2nd ed. Boston: Little Brown and Co., 1990.

Gorman, Robert. *Basic Text on Labor Law.* St. Paul, Minn.: West Publishing Co., 1976.

Hart, Henry, Jr., and Albert M. Sacks. *The Legal Process: Basic Problems in the Making and Application of Law.* Westbury, N.Y.: Foundation Press, 1994.

Levine, Peter. *Baseball History: An Annual of Original Baseball Research.* New York: Stadium Books, 1990.

Lowenfish, Lee, and Tony Lupien. *The Imperfect Diamond: The Story of Baseball's Reserve System and the Men Who Fought to Change It.* New York: Stein and Day, 1980.

Miller, Marvin. *A Whole Different Ball Game: The Sport and Business of Baseball.* New York: Birch Lane Press, 1991.

Monteleone, John J. *Branch Rickey's Little Blue Book.* New York: Macmillan Publishing Co., 1995.

Novak, Michael. *The Joy of Sports.* New York: Basic Books, 1976.

Rader, Benjamin G. *Baseball: A History of America's Game.* Chicago: University of Chicago Press, 1992.

Sands, Jack, and Peter Gammons. *Coming Apart at the Seams: How Baseball Owners, Players, and Television Executives Have Led Our National Pastime to the Brink of Disaster.* New York: Macmillan Publishing Co., 1993.

Seymour, Harold. *Baseball: The Golden Age.* New York: Oxford University Press, 1971.

————. *Baseball: The Early Years.* New York: Oxford University Press, 1990.

————. *Baseball: The People's Game.* New York: Oxford University Press, 1990.

Sommers, Paul M. *Diamonds Are Forever: The Business of Baseball.* Washington, D.C.: The Brookings Institution, 1992.

Spalding, Albert G. *America's National Game.* New York: American Sports Publishing Co., 1911.

Spink, J. G. Taylor. *Judge Landis and Twenty-Five Years of Baseball.* New York: Thomas Y. Crowell Co., 1947.

Voigt, David Quentin. *American Baseball.* 2 vols. University Park, Pa.: Pennsylvania State University Press, 1992.

Waller, Spencer Weber, Neil B. Cohen, and Paul Finkelman. *Baseball and the American Legal Mind.* New York: Garland Publishing, 1995.

Ward, Geoffrey C., and Ken Burns. *Baseball: An Illustrated History.* New York: Alfred A. Knopf, 1994.

Weiler, Paul, and Gary Roberts. *Sports and the Law.* Westbury, N.Y.: Foundation Press, 1993.

Weistart, John, and Cym Lowell. *The Law of Sports.* Charlottesville, Va.: Michie Co., 1979.

White, G. Edward. *Creating the National Pastime: Baseball Transforms Itself 1903–1953.* Princeton, N.J.: Princeton University Press, 1996.

Wilson, John. *Playing by the Rules: Sport, Society, and the State.* Detroit: Wayne State University Press, 1994.

Woodward, Robert, and Scott Armstrong. *The Brethren.* New York: Simon and Schuster, 1979.

Yasser, Raymond, James R. McCurdy, and C. Peter Gopelrud. *Sports Law Cases and Materials.* 3rd ed. Cincinnati: Anderson Publishing Co., 1997.

Zimbalist, Andrew S. *Baseball and Billions: A Probing Look inside the Big Business of Our National Pastime.* New York: Basic Books, 1992.

Zoss, Joel, and John Bowman. *Diamonds in the Rough: The Untold History of Baseball.* Chicago: Contemporary Books, 1996.

Index